# LEICESTERSHIRE & RUTLAND RAMBLES

## Fourteen Country Walks
## around Leicestershire & Rutland

Bryan Waites

———

With Historical Notes

COUNTRYSIDE BOOKS
NEWBURY, BERKSHIRE

*Countryside Books' walking guides cover most areas of England and Wales and include the following series:*

*County Rambles*
*Walks For Motorists*
*Exploring Long Distance Paths*
*Literary Walks*
*Pub Walks*

*A complete list is available from the publishers*
*3 Catherine Road, Newbury, Berkshire*

First Published 1992
© Bryan Waites 1992

COUNTRYSIDE BOOKS
3 Catherine Road
Newbury, Berkshire

ISBN 1 85306 130 1

Cover photograph:
Scene near Knossington taken by Andy Williams

Produced by MRM Associates Ltd., Reading
Typeset by Paragon Typesetters, Sandycroft, Chester
Printed in England by J. W. Arrowsmith Ltd., Bristol

To a very dear walking companion
and the spirit of Rutland

## Acknowledgements

Grateful thanks to Mr. Hinch
and Greetham Valley Golf Club

# Contents

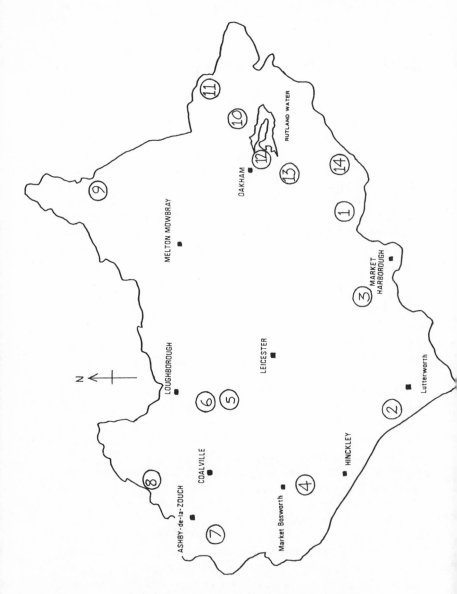

Sketch map showing locations of the walks

# Introduction

Despite Leicestershire and Rutland becoming united as one county in 1974, both areas remain relatively unknown and hidden in the midlands of England. Yet, to its natives and those visitors willing to stay awhile, the county has remarkable charm, attractiveness and character as well as a certain uniqueness. Indeed, to summarise, it has an intrinsic quality of real 'Englishness'. This is best discovered on foot and the intention of the walks included is to introduce the visitor and re-vitalise the native to Leicestershire and Rutland's highlights as well as the secrets of the landscape.

Full directions are given for each circular walk and details of distances, times, parking and refreshments. There are always bound to be some changes in the field but I hope these will be few and surmountable and that the walks have been kept fully clear.

We are lucky in Leicestershire as the County Council has vigorously launched its 'Waymark 2000 Project', in association with the national Countryside Commission Campaign, to signpost 3,000 miles of footpaths and public rights of way by the year 2000. This will improve public access to the countryside, in particular, drawing attention to beautiful walks of which the public may be unaware.

Additionally, the Country Landowners Association has warned farmers not to plough up rights of way but to make sure that all routes are wide enough — footpaths 1 metre, bridleways no less than 2 metres. The Regional Secretary said: 'It is in the farmers' own interests to see that paths are kept open', and, indeed, the Rights of Way Act 1990 gives councils greater powers of entry to private land where they can open up blocked rights of way and prosecute offenders.

Walkers will, therefore, have more assured routes to follow with full rights to do so. But remember your responsibilities also to follow honestly the Country Code and respect the countryside and its people. Remember also that walking along a footpath fills the bill entirely when it comes to keeping fit — and it doesn't cost anything! So keep walking and keep fit!

Bryan Waites
March 1992

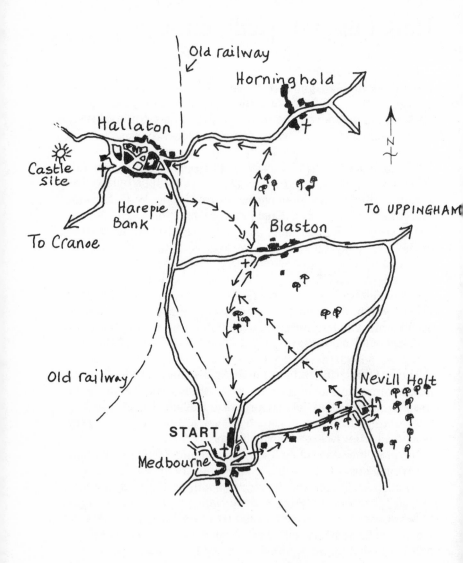

# Hallaton and Medbourne

**Introduction:** Hallaton and Medbourne are two of the most beautiful villages in Leicestershire. The latter lies on the edge of the Welland valley and the former only 2 miles north. History is all around and the landscape holds many secrets waiting to be discovered.

The line of the old Roman road from Leicester towards Godmanchester and thence to Colchester, can still be followed as it runs just south of Medbourne. According to W G Hoskins 'Medbourne is the only village in the county which can claim to have existed in Roman times as a minor settlement, apart from the villa or country house just outside it. As such, and as the last village in Leicestershire to lose its open fields, Medbourne would repay a special study'.

Both villages have imposing churches and lovely little walks within the confines, especially the riverside walk in Medbourne. Old buildings with a mixture of ironstone, brick and thatch abound and the green with its odd Butter Cross at Hallaton is a gem.

The walk describes a figure of eight as it starts in Medbourne, makes for nearby Nevill Holt, thence to Blaston and over the fields towards Horninghold but just turning to Hallaton before reaching that village. The return is via a field path to Blaston and then the field road from Blaston to Medbourne.

Nevill Holt hall and church form a memorable sight overlooking the Welland valley. It is a place you will want to cherish forever. Blaston's charm and its old ruined church by the river are also notable. If you can arrange to be in Hallaton on Easter Monday you can watch or take part in the traditional and hectic bottle-kicking contest which takes place each year. This struggle is between Hallaton and Medbourne on the river meadows south of Hallaton. But first, you must partake of a slice of the famous and gigantic hare pie served at the Hallaton rectory.

**Distance:** About 7 miles of varied walking with some outstanding views en route. Allow time to look round the villages and if you do so the walk will take about 4 hours. OS Landranger 141.

**Refreshments:** In Medbourne there is the Nevill Arms delightfully situated near the stream and bridges. In Hallaton, overlooking the green, is the Bewicke Arms, and a little distance away the Old Royal Oak and the Fox Inn at the north end of the village.

**How to get there:** From the A47, turn off at the sign to Hallaton which is 5 miles from Uppingham and 14 miles from Leicester. From the A427, turn off at Stoke Albany for Ashley and then Medbourne. Parking is possible near the church on the road outside and also at the Nevill Arms if you are patronising the pub. Market Harborough is the nearest town.

**The Walk:** Opposite the church you will find Rectory Lane and a public footpath sign. Walk between several fine houses and then between two stone walls as your path begins to narrow and to turn into a greenway. Go through the kissing gate which takes you over the old disused railway track and to another kissing gate. Cross the main road carefully to the stile into the pasture field ahead (sign). Follow the telegraph poles uphill to the left passing the corner of a house garden. At the top of the hill look back for a wonderful view over east Leicestershire.

Now cross a patch of rough ground and make for a small gate in the wall ahead. Keep to the left of a house you now see and go over to the drive, again bearing left towards the exit gate of the house leading to the road to Nevill Holt.

As you emerge from the gate and drive, turn right and walk uphill and you come to a fine avenue of trees, wrought iron gates and a gatehouse on the left. This is the entrance to the Nevill estate.

At the T junction, turn right for a short distance until you reach another set of wrought iron gates leading to the hall. Turn left through these to walk along the drive in front of the hall and church. The complex is now Nevill Holt prep. school but you are walking a recognised right of way. Cross the second stile you see on your right and follow a path which leads round the stable block via a gravel path. You pass through a wooden gate to reach this and then you see a footpath sign.

Join the main village street which is usually serene and quiet and like a scene from the distant past. You may have time to look inside the church and peep into the stable arch area. Turn left at the end of the village street and rejoin the main road near the telephone box and look for the bridleway sign at the other side of the road.

Go over the stile here and aim for another bridle gate at the far corner of the field, diagonally away from you. Go through the gate and follow the hedge line keeping it to your left. You walk downhill and soon come to the B664 Medbourne to Uppingham road. Cross this and over an arable field in front of you until you arrive at a bridge over a stream. Cross this and turn sharp left to a hedge leading uphill to a square spinney on the hill top. Walk with the hedge on your right, for one field, towards the spinney, then turn left aiming for an isolated tree on the skyline in the left-hand corner of the field. Find a gap to the right of the tree which leads to a hedge on your right. Keep this hedge on your right as you walk downhill to join a field road from Medbourne to Blaston.

At the field road, turn right and walk towards Blaston passing the lovely church in the river meadows to your left. Your route now lies along the gated road to Horninghold which you find signposted as you bear left away from the village. However, you will want to spend a little time in Blaston before resuming this route.

When you are ready, follow the gated road until you reach the main Hallaton to Horninghold road. Here, turn left to Hallaton, 1 mile away. When you reach the village, again, you will want to stay awhile. When you are ready to move on, take the Medbourne road out of the village and go for about ½ mile until you see a small wooden gate on your left and a signpost indicating a public footpath to Blaston. As this may be obscured you must look carefully for it.

Climb a wooden fence and go across a small field to a stile in a wire fence. Cross to the telegraph pole opposite and double gate over a stream (concrete bridge). Turn right into a large arable field and follow a grass track to the left of a hedge, with a telegraph pole on your left. At the corner of the field go through a large metal gate into parkland pasture. Now go diagonally across to the middle telegraph pole looking back from time to time for excellent views of Hallaton. You may spy the spire of Nevill Holt church on the far horizon. In front of you you will see the little Blaston church in the middle distance. Go across to join the field road you see on your left. This is the road you walked on earlier. Follow the avenue of trees on the road until you reach the Blaston-Hallaton road. Turn left, and after 100 yards turn right at the sign 'Field Road to Medbourne 1¾ Miles'. Follow this field road for your journey back to your starting point. You will join the B664 which will take you into Medbourne.

## Historical Notes

**Medbourne** is a place of great antiquity. Many Roman finds, especially to the west of the present village, indicate a large market centre with the Gartree Road to the south and possibly another Roman road coming in from the Nevill Holt direction. Huge numbers of coins have been found, as well as mosaics, pottery, slag, ovens, gullies and other stone features. All this indicates much more than a villa site. Also, profuse Anglo-Saxon finds show a strong continuity on the same site.

St Giles sits prettily at the riverside with a three-arched medieval footbridge to the west. According to some authorities, the church is 'lopsided' as if an ambitious new building programme had been started and then left uncompleted. To the rest of us we should be well satisfied with its stately and homely beauty. The actual site shows all the signs of age with its circular enclosure, but the present church dates from the late 13th century. After being destroyed by fire in 1270 it was rebuilt and completed about 1320 but the tower was added about 1370-1400. Much restoration took place between 1873 and 1912, the church once being described as 'perhaps the most dilapidated in the Diocese'.

Medbourne is only a mile or so from the Northamptonshire border which is marked by the river Welland and, of course, this river was a major route of entry for invading settlers advancing from the Wash in earlier times. To the east of the village the embankments and cuttings of the former Melton to Stamford railway can be seen and followed. To the west, the line branched towards Market Harborough. Now all is quiet along these disused lines but at one time they must have effected a minor revolution in the village since it sat in the triangle they formed on each side.

**Nevill Holt** was originally known as Holt (wood) and the patron as shown in the Bishop's Register of 1120-35 was Robert de Nevill, hence the acquisition of the prefix. In 1918 the hall was bought by the Rev C A C Bowlker for use as a preparatory school and the rest went to various farmers.

The church and hall form an integrated whole of majestic and harmonious proportions. There is some Tudor building and the earlier oriel window of 1476 is outstanding. The porch built by Sir Thomas Nevill is dated 1635 and inside the church there are Nevill family memorials. There are some lovely doorways and arches and an air of faded elegance adds charm to the whole scene as it sits high above the Welland valley. When the school is on holiday is the best time to visit and to peep into a few windows, very discreetly, of course.

In 1728, the village became a spa, and certainly one feels much invigorated by the salubrious air around and its apparent purity. It was the waters, however, which were said to be 'efficacious in all acute feverish and inflammatory diseases'.

**Blaston** is a charming and attractive village nestling in a side valley of a stream flowing to the river Welland. The ruins of the old church are near the Manor House down by the river, whilst the more recent chapel is situated in the meadow outside the village. It is always Sunday in Blaston and, although commuters undoubtedly hide away behind their modernised 17th century frontages, they are rarely seen. Another road once ran north beyond the old Blaston Hall (demolished in 1930) aiming for Hallaton, but it was often impassable and so the present street was extended. There are a number of very pleasant houses and cottages such as Crane's Cottages (1647 restored 1907); Thatch House (1617 restored 1907) and Stone House, but the whole village street is vintage England. Sir Malcolm Sargent once lived in Blaston.

**Hallaton** is a large, attractive village set amidst lovely, rolling countryside. Like Medbourne, its village stream eventually reaches the Welland and the same disused railway ran to the east. No wonder the villages were competitors (as the bottle-kicking shows) because they are only 2½ miles apart and one could stop up the headwaters of the stream if they so wished. Also, both towns had markets — was there room for this so close? Until 1953 you could get on the train at Hallaton too. I should think that the people of Medbourne thought they were too big for their boots in Hallaton — always one up.

After all, Hallaton had its famous Butter Cross set in a lovely green. Three pubs, at least. A small lock-up, a duck pond and best of all one of the finest motte and bailey castles in the county, now an impressive site and within easy walking distance. Not only that, but there may have been ironworking in the vicinity. Added to all that, despite Medbourne's appeal, Hallaton has many more old houses with thatch dating from the 17th century and a brick house of 1691. Who could ask for more? Yet there is more, a delightful and authentic museum with agricultural implements, tools, machines, documents, photographs and archaeological finds (Hog Lane, open weekends and Bank Holidays).

St Michael's has a most imposing west tower with a broach spire of the 14th century with a fine octagonal pinnacle.

**Bottle-kicking** takes place near the stream between Hallaton and Medbourne each Easter Monday. A huge hare pie is cut and distributed at the rectory in Hallaton then a battle commences for the possession of two wooden bottles or casks which are filled with beer. This may be a pagan custom, it could have been associated with the demarcation of parish boundaries or it might just have been a game — perhaps the forerunner of rugby? Further details can be found in Hallaton village museum.

# Fosse Way and High Cross

**Introduction:** High Cross was regarded as the centre of Roman England. Watling Street, from London to Chester, crossed the Fosse Way, from Exeter to Lincoln, at this point. They still do, and you can have a walk along one of the best surviving sections which remains, north east of High Cross.

High Cross is about 13 miles from the other High Cross in the centre of Leicester. The Fosse Way made its way to the town, crossing the river Soar and then aiming for Willoughby-on-the-Wolds before crossing the Trent at Newark and then arriving in Lincoln.

A significant Roman settlement called Venonis was located at High Cross and many finds have been made, though as yet no major dig has taken place here. Keep your eyes open in the fields and along the Fosse Way, you may be lucky enough to find a tile, coin or pottery.

Although your walk along the Fosse Way will be a gentle stroll in a leafy lane, you do suddenly find yourself at a good vantage point when you reach High Cross, which is some justification for the Roman engineers choice of road junction. You will see the beautiful heart of south west Leicestershire which is bounded for miles by Watling Street acting as county line. The walk takes you more deeply into this via Claybrooke Magna and Frolesworth and the small streams you may see and cross are the headwaters of the river Soar flowing eventually to the Trent and then the Humber estuary. In fact, you are walking very close to one of the major watersheds in England, with streams like the Swift and Avon to your south flowing to the Severn; the Welland flowing to the Wash as well as the Soar northwards to the Trent. Perhaps being on top of the world, English style, both historically and geographically, will make you feel even more invigorated than usual!

**Distance:** A total of 5½ miles of gentle walking with undulating scenery towards the end and perhaps a little rough land if the farmer has not tidied it yet. Allow 3 hours. OS Landranger 140.

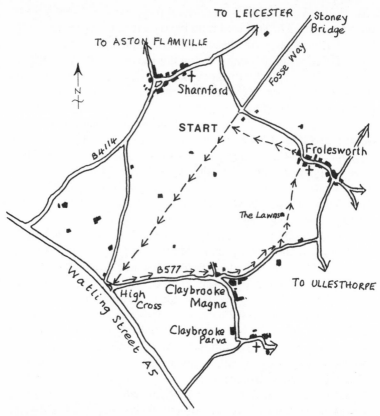

**Refreshments:** The Bulls Head and Woodcutter in Claybrooke Magna and the Plough & Harrow, Frolesworth.

**How to get there:** Leave the M69 at junction 2 for Sapcote and Sharnford. Just before reaching Sharnford turn left to Frolesworth. About ½ mile further on turn right at a minor crossroads. You are now on the Fosse Way. Carry on for almost ½ mile over a bridge and you will see a sign 'Unsuitable for Motors' on the left. Opposite, hidden behind a hedge, you will find a very pleasant and spacious car park in a field. Next to it there is a picnic area with tables. From the A5 turn off at High Cross following signs to Claybrooke Magna and Frolesworth. About 1 mile out of Frolesworth on the Sharnford road turn left at the minor crossroads. This is the Fosse Way. Another possible approach is from Leicester via the A46 then the B4114 to Sharnford turning off to Frolesworth as advised above until you reach the Fosse Way car park.

**The Walk:** Turn right leaving the car park, passing Cottage Farm on your right. The surfaced road bends left to Claybrooke Lodge Farm but you carry on ahead to the rough track with a footpath sign. There is no difficulty following the Fosse Way as it goes to High Cross and the distance is about 2 miles. You will pass through several kissing gates and the track becomes narrow in places but it is very attractive with shady, arched tree-lined sections. To each side you will glimpse, from time to time, arable and pasture fields and about halfway through there is Sharnford Lodge Farm on your right. If you observe the track very carefully you will see a cobbled surface and ditches at the sides. In some places the track is raised up above field level, especially noticeable to your right. There are excellent views to the south and south-east. Look for the tower of Frolesworth church.

As you reach the main road you will find a very helpful information board giving details of the Fosse Way, on your right. If you turn right here and go a short distance down Bumble Bee Lane you will come to the lovely High Cross Guest House on your left. Just next to this is the High Cross monument.

Now return to the information board to read about it and then proceed left down the hill into Claybrooke Magna on the B577, 1 mile away. The welcoming sight of the Bulls Head inn comes into view and you can call in for a pint of Marston's Pedigree in the garden behind the inn.

Take the road on the left for Frolesworth and in ½ mile you cross a stream which is one of the river Soar's most distant tributaries. There is a notice on your right 'Claybrooke Mill: Agricultural Merchants & Flour Millers'. A little further on you will see a footpath sign on your left at an iron gate. Go on to the path keeping to the left of the hedge. Look for the signs and yellow markers all along this part of the route.

In the far right-hand corner of the field cross a stile (marker) then in a few yards, another stile. Keep to the left following a wooden fence and aim for the corner of the pasture field with a stile and sign attached. Cross the stile on the left to yellow marked posts. Next go over a stile and plank bridge which leads into a pasture field. Cross the field diagonally towards the white house (The Lawns) on the hill top. Go through a small metal gate leading to the drive and close to the house. Excellent views if you look back to the Claybrookes.

Turn right, crossing a cattle grid, along the drive for 100 yards to a stile in the wire fence on your left. Cross into the pasture field to a yellow marker post with Frolesworth ahead, ½ mile away. Go on to a plank bridge and stile in the hedge opposite. Good views to the north west. Keeping to the hedge on your left, cross rough pasture to the corner ahead. Climb double stiles with plank bridge then go diagonally as indicated by arrows with a large duck pond on your left.

Go over to the marked stile in the hedge opposite. At the double stile cross and again go diagonally right through the field towards the bungalows on the skyline aiming for a yellow marker post at the far side.

You emerge on a grassy track between two fields. Turn right to the village of Frolesworth with one final look back over the landscape you have covered.

Bear left on the track, with the church well to your right, between houses on to the main street of the village with White Cottage opposite. You may want to spend some time looking round the church and village. However, to continue your walk, remember to turn left with White Cottage opposite you and in 100 yards you come to a footpath sign at a farm entrance. Go down the concrete drive and cross a very rough pasture field which I hope the farmer will have cleared by the time you use it. Aim for a gap in the hedge opposite, to the right of an ash tree. Cross a low fence and plank bridge into an arable field. Go across the middle of this field to the far side. If a crop is growing a path is usually easily visible through it. Look back for a view of Frolesworth on a terrace above river levels.

Keep straight on crossing another arable field to a gap in the hedge opposite, over a fence and directly across to a large tree forming part of a line of trees in front of you which is the Fosse Way. Much of the time you will see a green barn and a red-roofed house diagonally to your right.

Exit the final field at a gap leading on to the Fosse Way. There is a sign here 'Public Footpath to Frolesworth' pointing back along your route. Turn left, over the small bridge, and then right into your car park.

**Historical Notes**

**The Fosse Way** was constructed about 45 AD and ran from Lincoln to Bath and Exeter. It was virtually straight for 200 miles. The stretch from Stoney Bridge to High Cross is one of the few sections to survive in the original form. At one time the Fosse Way marked the frontier in Roman Britain. It rises gently to High Cross on Watling Street, the most important Roman road in Britain running from London to Chester, reaching 443 ft above sea level. Hereabouts there was a military township and market centre called Venonis or Venonae believed to have been sited on an existing Iron Age settlement.

Using your maps, it is interesting to note that the Fosse Way has been used throughout history to mark boundaries and you will find many parish, district and county boundaries follow this line.

**High Cross Pillar** is the remains of a monument erected by the Earl of Denbigh and others in 1712 marking the centre of Roman England and it was placed on the site of a wooden cross which stood there for many centuries. A larger and more ornate structure was situated in the centre of Watling Street near its junction with the southern Fosse Way but in 1791 it was wrecked by lightning and the remnants were re-erected in the present position. Leicestershire County Council have plans to enhance or replace the monument in the near future.

**Claybrooke Magna** was described by Lord Torrington in 1793 as 'large and populous and where the worsted trade whirls away'. Now it is a quiet place devoted to commuters who find it very handy near the A5. Actually, Claybrooke Parva, only just down the road, should be taken with Claybrooke Magna — they form a set. St Peter's church has a lavish and memorable chancel of about 1340 though most of the church is earlier, about 1300. The hall is opposite the church and dates from 1846. The name means brook or stream running over a clay bed.

**Frolesworth** stands above the river levels on a hill and its church of St Nicholas is a landmark around here. It dates from the late 13th and early 14th centuries though the top of the tower was rebuilt in 1762. Do not miss the Almshouses built in 1725 by the Rt Hon John Smith, Lord Chief Baron of the Exchequer for Scotland, who was born in the village in 1656. Make a point of seeing the quadrangle inside.

# Foxton Locks

**Introduction:** The canal revolution has left a wonderful legacy for walkers in Leicestershire. Following the canal network gives a quiet serenity away from the bustle of busy roads. Moreover, there are spectacular remains to be seen: beautiful brick bridges, aqueducts, cottages, inns, locks, inclined planes, reservoirs and canal feeders, tunnels, wharves and tramways. Added to this are the lovely narrow boats which give so much colour and life to the waterways today.

Foxton Locks is one of the outstanding sights in Britain. It comprises a staircase of 10 locks which lift the canal 75 ft and enable the Grand Union Canal to complete the last link 'in the great line of canals which extend from the Thames to the Humber'.

It is a most photogenic place and has constant interesting activity to watch. A pleasant short walk across nearby fields brings you to Gumley, once described by Arthur Mee as 'perhaps the prettiest village in the county, set amid steep hills and dales' and certainly the beauty of the countryside around and the exquisite walk up the village street to the church are outstanding.

A track leads from the village through open parkland and rolling countryside until it reaches and follows Saddington Reservoir which sends out feeders for the canal. Crossing the fields through pleasant valleys and fox coverts you can follow a canal feeder until it leads you to the main canal itself.

From here you make for Smeeton Westerby over the fields and then Debdale Wharf, once a thriving trading point on the canal in the 1790s. From here you simply follow the canal towpath to Foxton Locks and your mind can now be free of all necessity for map-reading and stile searching so that you can dream along in pleasant contemplation, as long as half a dozen cows and one sheep do not stray on to the towpath in front of you!

**Distance:** Generally a level walk with just a few uphill stretches near Gumley. Don't be daunted by the 8 miles which are full of

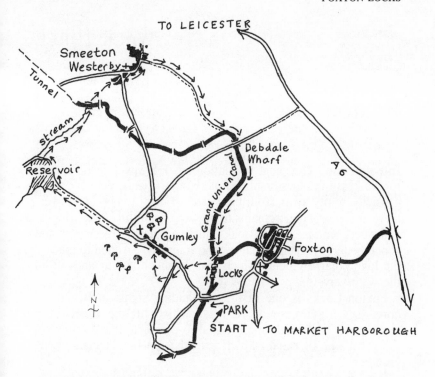

delights and surprises and will take about 4 hours. OS Landranger 141.

**Refreshments:** At Foxton Bottom Lock there is a shop and the Bridge 61 pub. In Foxton village itself, a short distance away there is the Black Horse inn and the Shoulder of Mutton. Gumley has the Bell inn.

**How to get there:** From Market Harborough take the A427 and turn off at Lubbenham or take the A6(T) out of town to the north and turn left to Foxton in just over 1 mile. Whichever route you take as you approach Foxton look for the sign to the Foxton Locks Picnic Park which has a small charge pay and display. There are toilets here, picnic tables and tree shade for cars. There is a ½ mile walk to the locks.

**The Walk:** From the picnic park follow the sign to the locks via a pleasant fir tree avenue. You reach the canal, go under the bridge, across a wooden footbridge and then you are on the far side of the canal. Walk to the Top Lock Cottage. As you go down the staircase of locks you will see the village and church of Gumley to your left.

Reach Bottom Lock by going under the bridge with Hall Brook Cottage on the left and Vagabond Cruises a little further beyond near the canal basin. Cross the footbridge over Bottom Lock and turn right up to a shop and toilets. There are useful booklets on the canal here. The canal museum is nearby.

Come out of the shop and turn right across the major bridge. Go through a metal gate with white markings on the top and nearby a bridle path sign. Follow a track for 100 yards until you reach another metal gate with yellow arrows. Cross a pasture field towards an isolated tree to the far right hedge following an indistinct path. Continue along the hedge line until you reach a wooden gate with yellow arrows. This brings you out on the Gumley-Foxton road.

Cross the road to the bridle sign opposite and pass through a metal gate into a pasture field to a small wooden gate which you can see on the opposite side. This comes out onto the Gumley-Lubbenham lane.

Turn left along the lane and immediately beyond the little bridge turn right at the sign into the field. Cross this field following the stream and hedge on the right for about 200 yards towards two tall ash trees. Just in front of these trees there is a plank bridge and stile which might be overgrown but is passable.

Enter the pasture field in front of you and make for the top power line walking uphill. Follow the power line up to the hedge and corner of the field. Go through the wooden gate (yellow arrows) and along a narrow path beside a house for about 100 yards until you reach the main street of Gumley (telephone box opposite).

Now go uphill along the main street and bear left past the church of St Helen and the clock tower of the hall stables (incidentally the clock is still working). Where the road divides take the left-hand lane signposted as a gated road to Laughton and Mowsley. Proceed for 200 yards and at a crossroads carry on forward into the gated road to Saddington. The village cricket ground and war memorial lie to your left in lovely parkland with delightful views. To the right at a little distance is an interesting house with topiary in the garden.

The lane to Saddington provides excellent views all around and gives a feeling of solitude and freedom. The hollow way at the start conveys a sense of the historical presence and the origins of this Anglo-Saxon village. A triangulation pillar at 165 metres emphasises the prominent position.

As you progress you will have ridge and furrow on your right for some distance, then Saddington village will appear about a mile away in front of you, on a hill. Eventually, as you pass Saddington Reservoir screened by trees on your left you will reach the dam and boathouse. Carry on past, downhill to the footpath sign, footbridge and stile on your right in about 150 yards.

Cross the footbridge and stile into the field and follow the hedge line until you reach a wooden and decrepit footbridge over the stream on your right. Cross over to footpath signs and turn left with a canal feeder stream on your right and the natural stream on your left.

Where the canal feeder begins to turn right look for a gap in the thistles which line the bank on your left. Walk towards a fence and cross a stile marked by yellow arrows into a pasture field with woodland to the left along a stream.

Make for a metal gate at the far end of this field. Go through and then across an old cart bridge over a small stream noting the tight meanders on your right. Follow the field path towards the woodland and on entering the tree belt turn right along a track to a canal aqueduct. Go under this but watch out for pools of water which sometimes collect here.

Cross the next field to a metal gate and then through a smaller field to another metal gate with the village of Smeeton Westerby visible in front of you. Cross the field diagonally making for a white board. Go over the fence, plank bridge and stile into the next field and then aim for the white house on the hill.

Go over the fence near the house where a footpath sign is located and into the village lane between houses. Follow the lane around to the left as it reaches the main road. Turn right until you are at the junction of Blacksmith's Lane and Debdale Lane. Turn right into Debdale Lane.

Debdale Lane is easy to follow as it crosses a field with wide views to the left and right, mainly across farmland. In about 1 mile you start to go uphill as you pass through a metal gate into sheep pasture and so, almost by surprise, you have reached the canal again. Cross the fence on to the towpath and note the recent demolition of a canal bridge.

Turn left and follow the canal towpath. Shortly you arrive at Debdale Wharf with its bridge (No.65) and canal basin, often with narrow boats moored there. Nearby there is a seat donated by 'Out and About' to commemorate the bicentenary of the Ordnance Survey 1791-1991. You have now an easy and pleasant walk for just over 1 mile alongside the canal to Bridge 62 which you cross to the Bottom Lock at Foxton. Make your way to Bridge 61 inn for a most welcome pint of Everards Original or a fresh orange and lemonade which you can sample on the seats outside overlooking one of the finest canal scenes you will ever encounter.

## Historical Notes

**Foxton Locks** were constructed on the advice of the great engineer Thomas Telford and built between 1808 and 1814. They are a miracle of early 19th century engineering. They are joined at the Bottom Lock by a branch canal from Market Harborough opened in 1809. When the link was finally made into Northamptonshire and the Grand Junction Canal at Long Buckby, a daily service could be offered to 'all parts of England'.

The intricacies of supplying water to the canal system alone deserves special study but, as with so many technological innovations, no sooner was the scheme completed than economic demands required improvements. Since it took at least 1 hour to navigate the staircase of locks a quicker alternative was devised, namely an inclined plane at the side. This was opened in 1900 but due to insufficient traffic it was also superseded and dismantled in 1911 even though it had reduced the transit time to 8 minutes.

Recent and continuing restoration and conservation work has made the entire lock system a very fine sight and the inclined plane has also been cleared so that the visitor can inspect it closely. The former engine house is now a museum. One of the most rewarding aspects is to look for the small details such as signs, nameplates, old machinery and the art forms associated with the great canal era. The narrow boats themselves provide intriguing details and a never-ending variety of names such as *Pocahontas, Ruddy Duck, Silver Shadow, Admiral.*

**Gumley's** church of St Helen has an unbuttressed west tower with a short broach spire of the 14th century. There has been extensive restoration in 1875-76. The nearby hall was begun in 1764 and demolished in 1964. It was built by Joseph Craddock, friend of Dr Johnson and David Garrick, the actor. Perhaps because of this connection, the house had a private theatre. The stable block of 1869 remains and it has an Italianate tower which seems totally out of character in this area.

**Smeeton Westerby** represents the linking of two separate settlements at some time in the past since Smeeton means 'smith's tun' or settlement and Westerby means 'west by' or village. Prior's map of 1777 marks two windmills which may suggest two separate hamlets.

**Debdale Wharf** is on the Grand Union Canal and though there is some marina activity it must be very quiet compared to its hey-day when it was an important coal wharf and, until 1797, the terminus of the canal. Then, in 1805, the Harborough branch was built.

**Foxton Village** is situated ½ mile from the famous locks but it is worth a visit. The church of St Andrew sits on an ancient hill site and the shaft of a Saxon cross in the fabric suggests a pre-Conquest origin. Though there are many later additions, much of the church dates from the late 13th and early 14th centuries. Look for the brass commemorating the village blacksmith who sang in the choir for 27 years – echoes of Longfellow!

Just beyond the Black Horse pub in Main Street you will come to a bridge and nearby there is the former blacksmith's shop (now a house) where canal horses could be shod. Here also there was a wharf where locally-made bricks were loaded into barges and coal imported. A weighbridge used by carters is at the entrance gate. It is said that bricks from Foxton were used to build St Pancras Station, London.

Other features to look for in the village are the old school, now a field centre, and the famous swingbridge which is turned for barges coming along the canal to allow them to pass. The old court house near the small green and close by the Baptist church of 1716 are interesting, especially as Foxton was a strongly Puritan centre.

# The Battle of Bosworth Field

**Introduction:** Would you like to re-live a great medieval battle and in the imagination, recreate the charge of a body of knights in full armour with their king at their head? This is possible at Bosworth Field where an award-winning re-creation of the events of 22nd August, 1485, has been successfully accomplished by means of trails, displays, films and models. Bosworth was a major turning point in English history ranking with Hastings and the Battle of Britain. It changed a dynasty and ended the Wars of the Roses by establishing the Tudors on the throne.

Our walk includes a battle trail and it visits the church at Sutton Cheney where Richard prayed the night before the battle. It passes through the parkland south of Market Bosworth to reach that ancient market town with its fine buildings and superb floral displays. The Ashby Canal provides a link which is followed as it anachronistically converges on the battlefield. Long boats now ply back and forth only 100 yards away from the place where Richard fell.

Battlefield, church, canal and famous market town comprise an unbeatable formula for the walker. Added to this is the beauty and charm of the west Leicestershire countryside often missed by the busy tourist hurrying along the impersonal motorways which skirt the area.

**Distance:** Six miles of easy and pleasant walking with the odd hill which could be done in 3 hours but you will need to allow extra time for studying the battlefield, visiting the battlefield centre and Sutton Cheney church and, perhaps, having a look around Market Bosworth. OS Landranger 140.

**Refreshments:** There is a cafe at the battlefield centre and at Sutton Cheney the Hercules inn and the Almshouse, beautifully situated behind the church. In Market Bosworth there are several inns and restaurants including the Dixie Arms, the Red Lion Hotel, the Forge and Bosworth Hall Hotel.

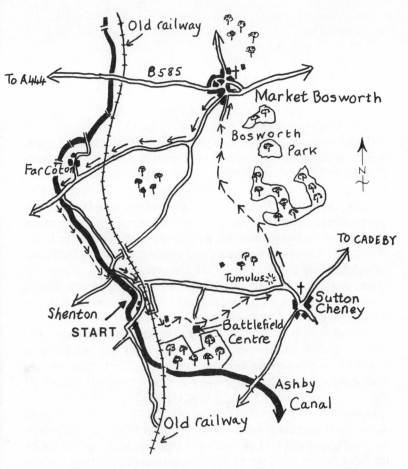

**How to get there:** From Leicester take the A47 to Hinckley but turn off at the B582 for Desford and Market Bosworth. From Hinckley take the A447 turning left on to the B585 for Market Bosworth. From the M42 leave at junction 11 down the A444 turning left for Market Bosworth along the B585. From the A5 join the A444 near Atherstone turning right for Market Bosworth in about 5 miles on to the B585. On arrival in Market Bosworth follow 'Battlefield' signs down Shenton Lane (off the market street) for 1½ miles, in the direction of Shenton. Do not go to Shenton but turn sharp left at the canal bridge and follow the lane round to Shenton station ½ mile further on. You will pass a lane signposted 'Battlefield Centre' but do not take this, carry on a little way to reach Shenton station on the left in a few minutes. Here you will find plenty of parking places and notice boards as well as toilets. The walk begins at the car park.

**The Walk:** Go over the railway and follow the path uphill, selecting 'Path 5 Battlefield Centre'. The route is easy to see and at the top of the hill on your right the royal standard of Richard III is often flying. This was the major area of the battle and information boards are well-placed to give you the details. The path bears right and at the top of the hill if you look left you will see Sutton Cheney church in the distance. You should have had lovely views towards Market Bosworth as you came up the hill.

As you reach the battlefield centre car park and picnic area turn left towards the centre for the cafe, shops, displays and exhibitions. To continue the walk, face the centre and then take the path to the left going over to wooden gates leading to a field. You can see Sutton Cheney church ahead. This is the walkers route. Do not turn into the main exit lane by mistake which is sharp left. You need to go straight ahead with the centre to your right.

Follow this path for several fields until you reach a car park about ½ mile away. Here you find another map board of the trails. Go out on to the main road and turn right and continue into Sutton Cheney to look in the church and perhaps, to take refreshment.

Return the way you entered the village and just past the Almshouse turn right into the gated road to Market Bosworth. Remember to close all the gates along this pleasant lane which leads eventually, after 1¾ miles, into the parkland on the edge of Bosworth Country Park. A final gate takes you into the town. Go to the end of this lane and then turn left into Shenton Lane, which will take you out of town. Walk down this lane for ½ mile to a lane forking off right to Far Coton. Continue along this lane for 1 mile until you reach a canal bridge. You will have passed a sign to Far Coton a short distance back but you should ignore this and follow the 'Sibson 3' sign to the humped-back canal bridge.

Once there, go down on to the towpath by crossing the bridge and turning left on to the towpath. Now follow this south for ¾ mile until you reach the aqueduct over the Shenton-Bosworth road. Fifteen yards beyond this aqueduct look for the steps which will take you down to the road below. They are on your right. Down the steps and under the aqueduct next, turning right at the sign 'Bosworth Battlefield Centre'. Do not take the road to your left marked with the same sign but go on a little and on your right you will see the path into King Richard's Field. Go in here to examine the stone erected where he fell. This is also a pleasant place for a picnic and you can go up a slope to the canal to see long boats moored alongside here.

Return to your car at Shenton station which is just across the road turning right out of King Richard's Field.

## Historical Notes

**Canal and Railway** run side by side here. Both are old friends for we keep coming across them time and again on our walks. The Ashby Canal has been described elsewhere (Walk Seven). At Market Bosworth it is about 1 mile west of the town and very pretty indeed at this point. Its close companion is the Ashby and Nuneaton Railway which we meet in the Moira area further north. This ran from the Ashby Woulds to join the London-Scotland main line at Nuneaton. Opened in 1873, it was closed to passenger traffic in 1931 and goods in 1981. It is extraordinary the way in which this line follows the canal, often being within a few yards of it. The Shackerstone Railway Society Ltd. operate their Battlefield Line, which is a steam-hauled passenger service, from Shackerstone to Market Bosworth, a distance of about 7 miles. There is a 'Railwayana' museum, shop, refreshment room, loco shed, etc, to visit as well as abundant car parking facilities at Shackerstone. The service operates at weekends and bank holidays. The 1 ¾ mile extension from Market Bosworth to Shenton station is nearing completion and it will be a great experience to arrive at the Bosworth battlefield by steam train in future.

**The Battle of Bosworth** was fought on 22nd August, 1485, and is still bright in the memories of many people, especially the supporters of the much maligned King Richard III who died bravely in combat. So much so that each year there appears in the Leicester Mercury under the Roll of Honour an insertion such as:

PLANTAGENET. Battle of Bosworth
August 22nd., 1485, killed fighting bravely
Richard III, King, soldier, statesman.
From present time,
Pale dusty ghost,
One grain of sand,
Salutes your memory, Trumpeter Sound!
*Leicester Mercury* 22/8/91

There are also services and events to mark the occasion, and of course, in 1985 the 500th anniversary was celebrated. Rightly so, for this battle is regarded as a major turning point in English history which brought to an end the Wars of the Roses and established the Tudors on the throne.

Henry Tudor, marching from Milford Haven where he had made his landfall, approached the scene of the encounter, perhaps via the Roman road from Mancetter. Meanwhile Richard III, in residence in Nottingham, heard of the landing and took up position in Leicester. He then left the town and moved along the ridge to Sutton Cheney. Here he is reputed to have heard mass for the last time. Nearby, at the tumulus at the gated road to Market Bosworth, he is said to have addressed and rallied his troops before the battle.

Richard then took up a strong position on Ambion Hill with marshland guarding his left flank. Though Henry Tudor was dismayed to see the glint of weapons from the King's considerable force of 12,000 men in a vantage point above him, he engaged the enemy fiercely with his mercenaries fighting bravely. However, the outcome might have been very different but for an incident which turned the tide in favour of Henry. The Earl of Stanley stood aside from the battle as a spectator with 6,000 men to the north, undecided which side to support. At the height of the battle, Henry rode with a body of men across to Lord Stanley's position, some say to persuade him to join the battle on Henry's side. Richard III, seeing this sudden move, thought that an attempt was being made to outflank him and charged down upon Henry with a company of his knights. A furious battle ensued and Lord Stanley decided to participate to such an extent that all was lost for the King. John Rous wrote 'If I may speak truth to his honour, although small of body and weak in strength, he most valiantly defended himself as a noble knight to his last breath often exclaiming that he was betrayed'.

This battle, described as 'the swan-song of chivalry', ended 30 years of family feud. This was the last time a King of England died fighting in battle, the end of the Middle Ages and the beginning of a new dynasty destined to make Britain great in the world.

**Sutton Cheney** became a prosperous place in the 19th century due to the canal opening up the area. There was some expansion of buildings and the church, previously more central, was set back from the new village street. St James is one of the most delightful churches you will encounter, and its setting, with the Almshouses of 1612 (now an hotel) is charming. Three periods of growth can be seen in the 13th century nave, the later chancel (much rebuilt in 1905) and the furnishings of the 18th century. Rough rubble walling in the south wall of the tower suggest an earlier building on this site. Inside are several interesting memorials. The oldest is to Margaret Neal dated 1567. That of Sir William Roberts, who built the nearby almshouses, is the most important — he died in 1633, and his coat-of-arms can be seen on the Manor House opposite the church. His tomb has been moved around the church and also defaced. Oddly, he is well-separated from his two wives who kneel together above him. Thomas Simpson, philosopher and mathematician, has a memorial, although he was not a local man. He died in 1761.

The most prominent position in the church is taken up by a modern memorial to Richard III erected by the Richard III Society and this is the focus for the annual memorial service held for the King.

**Market Bosworth** is in sight from the battlefield, especially on the walk up Ambion Hill. The spire of St Peter's being the best landmark. In the town today, one is struck by the magnificent floral displays due to the 'Britain in Bloom' successes over the years. Also the busy market has a neatness and sense of enclosure which contributes to a feeling of well-being. At first many surrounding buildings appear 19th century but on closer inspection several will be seen to be much older with timber framing, not always visible at first. The varied heights of the buildings enrich the townscape and Dixie Grammar School (re-founded in 1828) contrasts well with the curved line of lower buildings to the south west. Particularly attractive are three 16th and 17th century cottages in the narrower part of the market.

Bosworth Park was purchased by Leicestershire County Council in 1970 and is now a very finely developed country park. Once it was the major domain of the Dixie family of Bosworth Hall. This building has a fine south front of 1680 and is situated on the earlier manor house site. St Peter's church is really associated with the hall but there is a lovely view to it up Church Street. The church was greatly rebuilt in the 14th century with some remodelling in the 15th century. The old rectory of 1690 was south of the church but this was demolished and a new rectory built in 1849 much further off from the church.

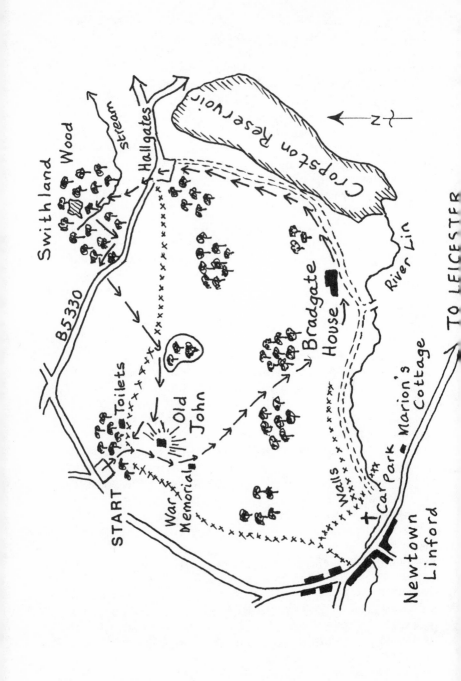

# Charnwood:
# Lady Jane Grey and Old John

**Introduction:** Charnwood Forest is not all forest but is a mixture of bracken-covered hills with craggy, dramatic rock outcrops, farmland, woodland, reservoirs, quarries, villages, deer parks and the M1 running right through the middle. It seems changeless but in fact it is everchanging. Yet for a long time it has been the lungs of Leicester providing vintage countryside recreation for many years to citizens who live only 7 miles away. They can be on top of Old John from the city centre within half an hour.

What a view they have! The Old John Tower stands nearly 700 ft above sea level and furnishes a panorama over all east Leicestershire and the city as well as more distant vistas. Millions of years ago this area was the site of a series of volcanic cones and even all this time later that earlier violence can still be seen in the sharp, angled rock outcrops. In fact, Charnwood is an alien area within the serene landscapes of Leicestershire, so much so that it has been considered a Wales in miniature or even a 'Little Switzerland'.

Who but the trained geologist could guess that after the volcanic action the area was later a desert and that even now clues such as fossil wadis can still be found.

This depth of geological interest is matched by a fascinating historical record, for close by the river Lin which traverses Bradgate Park is the ruined home of Lady Jane Grey — the nine day's Queen of England. Additionally, there is an interesting monastic influence in the area, sustained to the present-day by the existing Mount St Bernard Abbey.

Industry and quarrying have made inroads into the area particularly around its margins and in Swithland Woods, a remnant of the original oak woods, there are very scenic but dangerous old slate quarries. At Bardon and Mountsorrel active quarries, mainly for road metal, are still in operation. There are many land use conflicts which the walkers will see in Charnwood.

This walk, which is fairly short, takes you from Old John to the river Lin and the ruins of Bradgate House thence alongside Cropston Reservoir and into Swithland Woods, returning up to Old John by a different route. For extra information you should visit Marion's Cottage, Newtown Linford where many publications on the area are available.

**Distance:** This is a 4½ mile circuit downhill, once Old John has been reached, with level walking alongside the river Lin and Cropston Reservoir and in Swithland Woods but a steep ascent back to Old John at the end, much of it through springy bracken-fringed pathways. Allow 2 hours, though you may want to ponder at several points like the ruins, to watch the deer and to contemplate the views. OS Landranger 129.

**Refreshments:** Nothing actually en route but you can make a short diversion either by foot during the walk or by car later to Marion's Cottage, Newtown Linford. Also there are several places in Newtown Linford including Bradgate Tea Rooms, the Bradgate Public House & Rest, the Newtown Linford inn, Grey Lady Rest and Johnscliffe Hotel. Shops available.

**How to get there:** Leave the M1 at junction 22 and follow signs to Markfield and Newtown Linford (B5327). On reaching the latter turn left on a minor road to Swithland and in 1 mile look for the Old John car park to the right where the road forks. There are toilets at the car park. From Leicester take the B5327 to Anstey and then to Newtown Linford. Go straight on and then bear right for the Old John car park.

**The Walk:** From the car park go through the gap in the stone wall on to the woodland track. Two hundred yards ahead you pass through a wooden gate, just to the right of the toilets. You see Old John in front and the steep green slopes favoured by skiers in winter. Walk towards the war memorial which is the pillar to the right of the Old John Tower but as you get nearer bear left and make for Old John. Climb up to the toposcope for the best view and use it to name the distant features.

Now go through the gap in the wall which surrounds the nearby woodland and leads to the war memorial. A gap at the far side of the wood lets you through to the memorial. From here you can see to the west. Return through the wood and make your way downhill away from Old John. Aim for the red river cliff in the middle distance below.

It does not matter really which path you take as long as you go downhill. You are going to reach the river Lin and the road alongside soon and then turn left to the ruin of Bradgate House. Now you will see the red cliff better. It is a remnant of a desert wadi and has been scoured out by the river action plus man using the material for brick-making. As you will notice, Bradgate House was one of the first unfortified brick-built country houses in the country, being started in 1490. Note also the Swithland Slate walls around.

Go along the road below the house following the river valley eastwards with Old John on your left on the skyline. You reach toilets on your right and now you walk alongside the Cropston Reservoir. In ¾ mile you come to the Hallgates car park with an information board. Exit the car park turning left at the main road B5330. Carry on for a short distance to Horseshoe Cottage Farm on your right. Immediately past the farm go over a stile with a footpath sign to Swithland. Cross over a pasture field diagonally to the far corner where you can cross a bridge and stile into Swithland Woods.

Turn sharp left to follow a track along the stream until you reach a large bridge in 100 yards. Turn left to cross this bridge and follow the bridle road for 200 yards through woodland to a gate.

Turn right into the car park located here and follow the track through the car park keeping fairly close to the wall on the left bordering the main road. Continue to the left of a litter bin and you soon come to a gap in the boundary wall. On the opposite side of the road you will see a sign showing the route to Old John. Cross the road carefully and proceed into the track with Old John clearly in view ahead of you. The wide track leads you to a kissing gate in the park wall. Once through this you can find your own route back to Old John and then return to your car by the same track as you approached via the gate in the wall and through the wood.

## Historical Notes

**Bradgate Park** was given to the people of Leicestershire by Charles Bennion in 1928. It was designated a country park in 1970 and extends over 850 acres. It is a magnet for tourists and visitors just as Rutland Water is on the east side of the county. In many ways, despite being only 7 miles from Leicester, it is a throwback to medieval times with heathland, bracken, woodland, grassland, craggy outcrops, ancient trees and herds of deer.

Bradgate was enclosed from the waste of Charnwood Forest to form a deer park, certainly before 1247. It was part of the Manor of Groby and owned by the Ferrers family. When Sir Edward de Grey was created Lord Ferrers in 1445 the estate passed into the line of this influential family, Sir John Grey married Elizabeth Woodville who, on his death married Edward IV. It was this connection which gave Lady Jane Grey the right to the throne since she was a direct descendant of Henry VIII on her mother's side.

Bradgate House, now a ruin, was begun in 1490 and completed about 1510. It was one of the first unfortified brick-built country houses in England. It may be that when the house was being constructed that the villagers of Bradgate were removed outside the park, though it might have been earlier. They were removed to the 'new town at Lin ford' now known as Newtown Linford, outside the main gate.

In the 17th century, the Greys were also created Earls of Stamford (1628) and continued to occupy the house until the 1740s when it began to be neglected. According to the Leicestershire historian Throsby, by 1789 it was in ruins. In 1805, another famous local historian, Nichols, wrote: 'The courts of this magnificent mansion are now occupied by rabbits and shaded with chestnut trees and mulberries'. The tenth and last Earl of Stamford died in 1976 and a commemorative oak was planted in the park.

A great deal of additional land has been acquired for the estate since 1928, in particular, Swithland Woods donated by Leicester Rotary Club in 1931. Thus, the total area of the *whole* estate is now over 1,254 acres and is managed by the Bradgate Park Trust. Much of the estate is a Site of Special Scientific Interest (SSSI).

**Old John Tower** was built about 1786 and some say it is a folly, others a hunting tower. According to custom, it was erected to commemorate an old retainer of the Greys who was killed by a falling maypole during a party. There is a toposcope nearby which indicates viewpoints all round.

**Cropston Reservoir** was under construction between 1860-70 with the intention of supplying water to Leicester. The river Lin flows into it. A total of 140 acres of farmland were flooded as was the Old Keeper's House.

**Swithland Wood** covers about 146 acres and is a remnant of the original oak woods of Charnwood Forest. There are many pathways in this beautiful wood and a rich and diverse flora and fauna. Birch and lime trees are also found. There are two water-filled slate quarries, now fenced round for safety. Much of the famous Swithland Slate used in the Midlands came from these quarries. In May each year a 'bluebell service' is held in the woods.

**The Geology of Bradgate Park.** The oldest and hardest rocks which appear as jagged crags are Pre-Cambrian and more than 600 million years old. Surrounding these are softer rocks called Keuper Marls, from the Triassic Period, 225 to 180 million years old. The former were produced under volcanic conditions as 'bombs', dust and ash covered the area issuing from several volcanoes to the north west. The latter were produced under desert conditions and continue to be eroded thus exposing more and more of the underlying ancient rocks. Before Triassic times, there was intensive folding and faulting of the rocks with the intrusion of molten magma which did not reach the surface at the time but can now be seen in several locations, for example, just inside the main gate (Newtown Linford entrance) and near the ruins. These are called syenites or Markfieldite, quarried in some local areas for road metal.

**Newtown Linford** is a linear village with timber-framed buildings as well as Charnwood 'granite' used in conjunction with dressed stone and brick. Roofs are often thatch or Swithland Slate. The medieval church, much restored in 1860, has some finely carved tombstones of Swithland Slate in the churchyard. Several old village pumps can be seen, one opposite the village stores. The streetscape is very attractive especially where the curve of the road blends in so well with the trees along it. The main disadvantage is that most visitors to Bradgate Park come to the Newtown Linford entrance or pass through the village on the way to other parts of Charnwood. This makes it very busy at certain peak times.

# Charnwood:
# Broombriggs and Beacon Hill

**Introduction:** Leicestershire is not noted for its mountains and although locals say that there is nowhere higher between Tilton-on-the-Hill and the Urals in Russia, as the crow flies, this is more due to the low lying land en route than the escalating heights of the county. Yet, in the right places, you can easily believe that you are in a mountainous area.

Such a place is Beacon Hill and, only ½ mile to the south, Broombriggs Hill. Over 800 ft in height, there are remarkable views over Loughborough and the Soar valley and in the distance Nottingham and the Goatham Hills can be discerned as well as the power stations in the Trent valley. Twenty miles to the east you will see, on a clear day, the great Jurassic escarpment which crosses the eastern corner of the county as it trends from the south coast to the Yorkshire coast. If your eye is keen enough you may pick out Belvoir Castle on the scarp. Perhaps you may also notice the BBC TV mast at Waltham On The Wolds and the isolated hill known as Billesdon Coplow, also located on the scarp. To the north west you will see, if you are lucky, the distant limestone hills of Derbyshire. Nearer, in the same direction, look for the ancient church of Breedon On The Hill. The toposcope on Beacon Hill will help you to locate many of these places but a map will help too. Perhaps you may be able to see Lincoln Cathedral on a clear day — some say it is possible — although it is 60 miles away!

The Broombriggs walk will live in your memory. It may well be one of the most outstanding in the Midlands for it combines magnificent views with a kind of quiet privacy as it meanders through arable, pasture and woodland. Since it partly includes a farm trail there are information boards which add to your understanding of the landscape.

If you want inspiration from the English countryside and a refreshment of the spirit then this is the walk you need.

**Distance:** This walk is shaped like a bow tied in the middle and

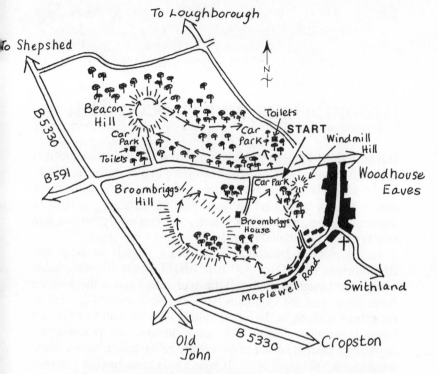

it is a total of about 5½ miles long. First you walk the Broombriggs section which is hilly in parts, then you cross the main road to walk up and down Beacon Hill. Allow 3 hours and take a picnic because the highest point on Broombriggs Hill has the most delightful place to pause and sit looking towards Leicester and Old John as well as most of east Leicestershire and there are seats and tables too. OS Landranger 129.

**Refreshments:** The Broombriggs leg of the walk emerges after ¾ mile on to Maplewell Road and close by you will find the Curzon Arms on the left with a very pleasant beer garden. Almost opposite is the Cottage in the Wood restaurant. In Woodhouse Eaves, only ½ mile further on there are several pubs and restaurants including the Forest Rock inn, the Griffin, the Pear Tree, the Wheatsheaf and Ye Old Bulls Head.

**How to get there:** Beacon Hill and Broombriggs are about 1 mile west of Woodhouse Eaves. From Leicester follow the A6 and turn off left at Rothley following the signs. From the M1 leave at either junctions 22 or 23 and also follow signs to Woodhouse Eaves/Beacon Hill which are only 1 mile away. When you arrive at the B591 road look for the Broombriggs car park which is close to the junction of the B591 and the Nanpantan road. Do not go into either Beacon Hill car parks.

**The Walk:** From the Broombriggs car park enter the handgate at the side and go along the fence to your right. Through a gate cross a pasture field to the yellow marker at the edge of woods ahead. You will find yellow markers all along your route. At this point, if you wish, you can turn sharp left and go up on to Windmill Hill, once the site of a prominent post-mill. Return to your original path and carry on to a bench near to a five bar gate. Go through this gate into a tree-lined path with walls on each side. Eventually, this becomes a surfaced road leading to the village street, Mill Lane. You pass a small butcher's shop and several lovely houses and gardens.

You reach the main road, Maplewell Road, where you must turn right. Carry on for about ¼ mile until you reach a bungalow on the left, No. 123, with very prominent conifers in the garden. Opposite there is a wooden handgate at the other side of the road. Go through this gate into a grassy area and then left through another handgate (yellow marker). Proceed uphill alongside a hedge keeping it to your right. Just before a telegraph pole ahead with a yellow marker on it, turn left up a grassy path at a marker post. Keep a wood to your right. Look for a pond half-hidden in the wood. There are lovely views back to Mountsorrel. Note the information board about crop rotation and the seat.

Carry on to the pinewood ahead with a seat nestling close to a stone wall. At the top of this hill is an outstanding view. Over a stile into a small walled enclosure with a seat and another information board on land use and quality. Go over the next stile into the pasture field beyond.

Keep the wood and stone wall to your right until you reach the top of the hill where you see the most glorious views in all Leicestershire, Old John fairly close and all of east Leicestershire plus the city. There are seats and picnic tables, and exquisite isolation. A board gives details on grasses you can identify.

Pass a five bar gate and go over the stile, both on your right. Keep to the right-hand wall of the field (markers) and where it bends cross the field diagonally to the marker post at the far side.

Cross a stile next to a gate here at the side of a wood and over to follow the wall to the left-hand corner of the field. Again, if you care to look behind you will have wonderful views of the city and a silhouette of Old John. Follow the fence and markers around the edge of the pasture viewing Ratcliffe power station in the distance. Note hay and silage board, picnic table and seats. Beaumanor Hall is in the trees in the middle distance below. Continue round the field with a wire fence to your left until you arrive at the far corner with handgate (markers) and noticeboard on walls and hedges.

Go into a wide grass track and walk along as it bears left to another handgate into woodland. Emerge on to a drive which leads to Broombriggs Farm which is often open to the public. Here you find a farm trail board. Go through the handgate nearby and follow yellow markers on tree pens in the field. Keep right of a small clump of trees following markers. Look for 'The Story of Broombriggs' noticeboard a little earlier. You come to a stile on your left. Go over and along a well-marked pathway round the field. Pass a noticeboard on cereals. Halfway round cross a stile, go to the far side of a pasture field where you see a yellow marker and open gate. This leads to your starting point at the car park.

If you feel you have had enough you need not walk the final leg up Beacon Hill. However, for those who wish to rise to greater heights, leave the car park and turn left on the main road. After a short distance you will see a gap in the wall on the opposite side of the road. Cross to this carefully and turn left at the bridlepath in the woods. In ¾ mile of uphill walking you arrive at the summit of Beacon Hill. Examine and enjoy the views by using the toposcope and look for the trig. point.

Now your return journey should be on the edge of the woodland on the opposite side from which you arrived passing on the way down Frying Pan Pond. Shortly after this you enter woodland for about 500 yards to arrive at the Beacon Hill car park on the Nanpantan Road. Take the path past the toilets and it will take you back to the gap in the wall and your original car park.

## Historical Notes

**Windmill Hill** is a wooded area above Woodhouse Eaves and it is owned by Leicestershire County Council. There was a post-mill here, so called because the upper part pivoted around a large central timber post so that the sails moved into the wind. This was damaged by a gale in 1895, restored, but then burnt down in 1945 so that only the stone base remains. Good views are possible since the hill is over 500 ft in height. To geologists this site gives evidence of volcanic ashes (Beacon Hill Beds) on the south west and south sides; ignimbrite (welded tuff plus pumice fragments) at the summit and downhill northwards grey, slaty, highly-cleaved rocks.

**Woodhouse Eaves** lies on the edge of your walk and its name also means on the edge of the forest. It is the daughter village of Old Woodhouse, a short distance to the east. Once, villagers had to walk to church in Old Woodhouse but in 1837 William Railton designed a new church located above an old quarry overlooking Woodhouse Eaves. He was the man who designed Nelson's Column. The village is a living embodiment of the geology of the area with its generous use of local stone and slates. It is interesting to observe the many different uses.

**Beaumanor Hall** can be seen during your walk from Broombriggs Hill. In 1974 it was purchased by Leicestershire County Council for use as an in-service conference and field centre. Previously, from the Norman Conquest until 1946 when the estate was sold, it had been the seat for a succession of aristocrats. First the Earl of Chester and later the Beaumont family who entertained Richard II and his Queen there. In the 16th century the Greys owned the Hall and in 1595 it was purchased by the Herrick family, associated with the famous poet, Robert Herrick. The present hall was built in 1847 and during World War II it was requisitioned by the army.

**Broombriggs Farm** was presented to Leicestershire County Council in 1970. It is mixed arable and stock with 139 acres. A network of paths together with information boards helps the public to understand the workings of a marginal farm in a tourist area and the problems it has. There is special access from time to time with events to see.

**Beacon Hill** is 818 ft high and is the second highest point in the county after Bardon Hill. A total of 213 acres comprising Beacon Hill were purchased by the County Council from the Beaumanor estate in 1946. Now the hill can be approached on all four sides. There is evidence that the hill was used in prehistoric times and, to some extent, the man-made contours on the slopes seem to show this. Because of its prominence, it is likely that an Iron Age hill fort was located here, similar to that at Burrough Hill in the east of the county.

The earliest discovery is a flat bronze axe of the early Bronze Age. The Hill is a scheduled ancient monument and it is an offence to damage it in any way or to use a metal detector in the area. One day archaeological excavations may take place which will reveal more details about its role in Leicestershire history.

From the summit of Beacon Hill can be seen the whole geological structure of Charnwood Forest. There is a huge fold of rocks which during the last 600 million years has been breached to leave a series of broken, horseshoe-shaped, parallel ridges of which Beacon Hill, Broombriggs, The Brand and Swithland Woods form a part. This ancient area of Pre-Cambrian rocks is one of the oldest in Britain and it is surrounded as a plain by younger rocks. For many years it was thought that no fossils would ever be found in the ancient rocks until a schoolboy discovered the oldest fossil in the world – *Charnia masoni,* named after him and 700 million years old.

On Beacon Hill itself, the crags can be seen to be striped in layers of green, grey and cream colours. Much of this is volcanic ash laid down in a sea. Several volcanic eruptions were involved, indeed, there may have been more than one volcano in action at different times. About 600 million years ago a mountain building episode tilted the rocks into their present craggy positions. Hardened volcanic dust and ash have been split into very sharp protrusions known locally as 'hornstones'. It is thought likely that there were a group of island volcanoes in a wide ocean area.

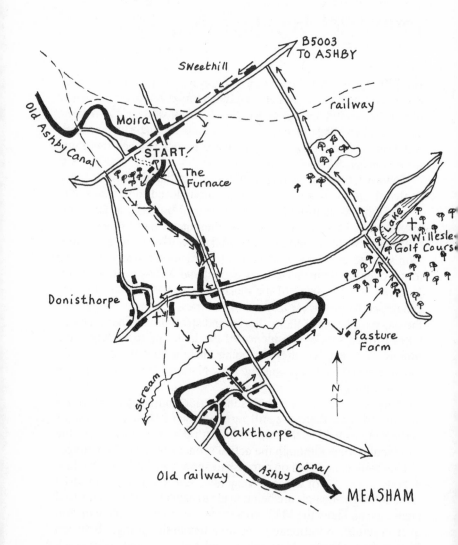

# Industrial Heritage Ramble

**Introduction:** North west Leicestershire is very different from the rest of the county. For at least 200 years it had been the centre of industry including coal mines, canals, tramways, brick-making, steam engines, blast furnaces, railways and the like. Its landscape was scarred and disfigured by industry in an era when there was little concern for the environment.

However, over the years this industry has changed and declined so that the last active collieries in the area closed some years ago. It is helpful to visit the Snibston industrial museum at Coalville to get some idea of the impact of mining on the district.

You can walk around the industrial graveyard between Moira, Donisthorpe and Oakthorpe partly along disused railway and canal to discover the remnants of a once great and wide-spread industry. You can stand in front of the blast furnace at Moira, follow the canal, see former wharves, pass by miners' cottages, walk over the old spoil heaps of the collieries and stroll beside the 'flashes', lakes formed by the subsidence of the land due to underground mining. You can see attempts being made to turn the dereliction into a restored landscape and the New National Forest is one hope for the future.

There is a fascination with this industrial landscape and its relics but amidst it all there are still farms, green fields, lovely walks and beauty as well as the odd architectural gem. There is still the spectacular view although the actual scenery may not be vintage.

This walk is included on purpose to show you the Leicestershire nobody knows — or at least, very few. For it is not yet a tourist area, although attempts are being made to capitalise on the industrial landscape and now the M42 crosses the area more people will stop over in future. Additionally, the area lies in the triangle between Birmingham, Derby, Nottingham and Leicester and so in reach of a vast population. Moreover, Ashby-de-la-Zouch and the Ivanhoe legend add a new dimension to it all.

**Distance:** About 6½ miles of fairly level walking, some over rough ground, so wear stout shoes and try to avoid wet days as the land may then be soft between Donisthorpe and Oakthorpe. Allow 3½ hours, perhaps even a little longer if you intend to pause at the Moira Furnace and Willesley Park. OS Landranger 128.

**Refreshments:** You pass the Mason's Arms, Donisthorpe, about one third of the way round your walk. In the village itself there are the Turk's Head and the Engine, whilst at Oakthorpe you will find the Gate, Hollybush and the Shoulder of Mutton. There are several pubs in and around Moira. You will find shops in Moira, Donisthorpe and Oakthorpe.

**How to get there:** From Leicester take the A50 to Ashby-de-la-Zouch then the B5003 to Moira. Look for signs to Moira Furnace where there is a car park. Access also via the M42/A42. Leave junction 11 and follow signs to Donisthorpe and Moira via the A444 and subsidiary roads. The walk starts at the Moira Furnace car park which is always available and free but there are no toilets and the furnace has only limited opening hours. To check opening times ring Ashby tourist information centre 0530-411767.

**The Walk:** Read the information boards around the Moira Furnace and study the site. Note the Ashby Canal close by. Go over the stile at the edge of the wood opposite the furnace. Do not go into the wood at the kissing gate. Keep close to the edge of the wood, to your right. Soon you see seven old lime kilns to your left and a pond too. At a yellow marker-post bear right over a stile. To your right, in the wood, is Engine House Cottage, earlier than the furnace, once used to house a steam engine which pumped water from mine shafts in the wood.

You emerge on to a wide track. Follow this to a yellow marker and arch in front of you. You have arrived at the now disused Ashby and Nuneaton Joint Railway. Turn left at the marker on to the surfaced lane, go past the houses on the left to a marker ahead. Make a small diversion right on to the disused railway line to see where the Moira-Ashby Woulds Heritage Trail starts and to read the information boards. This trail is part of the County Council's 'Landmark' scheme to improve the environment and walkways in Leicestershire. Poplar Avenue, on the other side of the railway, was a miners' row and used to be called Snailhouse Row.

Return to your original side of the railway and follow the track in front of you as it narrows between high hedges. You come to a yellow marker-post on the right. Turn right here towards two large concrete posts which once supported a footbridge over the canal at this point. You are back on the course of the old canal.

Go to the marker-post ahead. Cross the stile at the marker-post on your right. Proceed into rough ground with Donisthorpe ahead. You are walking on the former spoil heap of Donisthorpe Colliery which is being flattened. Keep close to the hedge on your left. The canal is on your left-hand side, but it has been filled in. Follow the line of telegraph poles to a yellow marker ahead. Donisthorpe church is over to the right in the distance.

At the marker cross a stile on to Moira Road below via a steep path through trees. Cross the busy road carefully to the other side and keep to the footpath. Note dates on houses are mainly 1902, 1903 and 1904. This is part of Donisthorpe even though it is situated some distance away from the centre. After 500 yards turn right at the Mason's Arms, signposted 'Donisthorpe ½ mile'. Keep to the footpath on the right past a large wheel at the recreation ground. Note houses on the opposite side of the road are below road level which indicates that there was a canal bridge here. Carry on past the cemetery and over the disused railway line bridge. As the road bends left look for the sign 'Public Footpath to Steam Mill, Oakthorpe', next to the church. Turn left and follow the path.

Pass through an open iron gate between a wire fence and hedge with the disused railway on your left. Oakthorpe is visible 1 mile ahead. Cross the disused railway bearing left. Keep to the path at rear of houses with their wire fence on your left. There is a large chimney to your right.

Cross low metal posts and continue to the left of the hedge line. There are two ponds (flashes) on your left indicating subsidence. You come to a footbridge with a lake which is a most lovely surprise and, although it seems to have gone astray somewhere, you have crossed Saltersford Brook.

Now walk uphill along a narrow track to Oakthorpe through a kissing gate. Keep to the left of a high hedge where the path leads clearly to a small wooden gate. Cross rough ground over former Ashby Canal noting this is Canal Street and also the Old School House on the right. At Windy Ridge bungalow turn left at a sign, going between houses via a very narrow path with hedges both sides.

After 100 yards cross an old stile (arrow) into a pasture field. Good views to the left of Donisthorpe church on a ridge and a former colliery. Follow the hedge around to your right. Turn left at the corner ahead and in 50 yards cross a stile to the busy Moira-Measham road. Directly opposite is a sign 'Public Footpath to Willesley' and a stile. Cross the stile into the field of thistles. Follow tree line and fence to steps and stile in the left-hand corner of the field. Make for the hedge diagonally left at farm and walk along with hedge on your left along the filled-in line of the old canal. Willesley Woods are ahead.

You pass a large, stagnant pond on your right and then go over a low wooden fence. The track continues through scrubland. At a barbed wire fence ahead near a double power line, find a stile which is a few yards to the right, behind a bush. Cross it into the site of abandoned mine buildings, now demolished but brick-strewn. Turn sharp right into a grassy track leading to Pasture Farm, ½ mile ahead.

At the farm track turn left between a hedge and a wire fence. Continue on the grassy track between bracken to an iron gate with a gap to the right side. Walk with the tree line to your right in the arable field. Where the field boundary turns left carry on along it until you reach the edge of the small wood on your right. Look very carefully here for a gap into the arable field beyond on the right. Walk across the large field diagonally left towards the left-hand side of a large wood with golf greens beyond. As a help, look for the yellow notice on one of the power lines and aim for 100 yards to the left of this, where you will find a gap in the hedge.

You reach the main road close to an entrance to the Willesley Golf Club. Do not go into this, but turn left along the main road. In 200 yards you reach a public footpath to Willesley Park and lake on your right. If you wish, you can walk the 500 yards up the path to see this lovely site with its church. The park is the Ashby and Coalville Scouts district camp site.

Return to the main road by the same path and turn right. You have woodland to your right for ¼ mile and the road crosses a small stream. At the crossroads carry straight on, signposted 'Moira 1½ miles'. This part of the walk is uphill for a short distance and you pass Wood Farm Cottages on your right. As you do, look to the far horizon on the right to see Ashby and the castle with the church next to it. If you look back downhill, you will see the busy traffic on the M42/A42 on the far ridge.

Coming this way gives you the chance to see derelict land, flashes, spoil heaps to the left, and opposite, a sign proclaiming the New National Forest, where many young trees have been planted. Cross the railway bridge ahead, the still active Leicester-Burton line. Good views from this bridge to west and south. Moira can be seen to the left in the middle distance.

At the main Ashby-Moira road turn left for Moira (signposted Overseal). Cross over to walk on the footpath. As you walk the next ¾ mile look out for typical features of a declining mining area such as wasteland next to housing, neglected areas, empty buildings, vandalism and attempts made by local authorities to reinvigorate community spirit. Sweet Hill will furnish examples of this. Behind it looms the abandoned mine apparatus of Rawdon Colliery with its gigantic spoil heap. Did you see the VR post box?

At the railway bridge turn sharp left and go down a lane behind the bridge which is hard to see at first. On your right you see the renovated Old Row, built in 1848. A little further on, to the left, there is the Machine House, once the place where coal was weighed before being transferred from the pits up here to the canal wharves by tramway.

Turn right at the Machine House down a grass track to a wooden fence marked with a yellow arrow. Cross the fence into the field and make for a waymarked stile opposite. Go into a grassy track between trees. At a yellow marker-post turn right into a woodland path which runs near the edge of the wood. As you emerge from the wood you are between hedges and it will now be clear to you that you are following an old tramway which took coal from the pits round the Machine House area known as Newfield, started in the 1830s and abandoned in the 1890s.

Soon a house comes into view ahead and the path may run through nettles here. You arrive at the main road from Measham to Moira at a bridge. You may notice a No. 4 on this which is a point on the Moira trail. If you can obtain a copy of this from the museum or Ashby tourist office you can find out much more. The bridge was over the tramway which you have just traversed.

Turn right for 100 yards. Cross the busy road to the footpath sign at the side of Secura Labels (which was once a canal wharf). Turn left into the field and follow the footpath to the bridge ahead which is next to the Moira Furnace. You are again following the Ashby Canal and at last you can see some water in it when you approach the furnace building. Turn right into the car park from where you began the walk.

## Historical Notes

**The Moira Furnace** was built about 1804 by the Earl of Moira who wanted to exploit the mineral wealth of the Ashby Woulds, close by. After the area was enclosed in 1800 the way was open for the Earl, who owned the land, to mine the coal reserves which were then used to smelt local ironstone. The Ashby Canal, next to the Moira Furnace, brought coal, ironstone and limestone from the Ashby Woulds and elsewhere. However, the furnace and foundry were under-used and largely restricted to serving the local market. The Coal Measure ironstone was poor quality and the coal too valuable to waste as coking coal for smelting, thus, by about 1812 it ceased operations. Nevertheless, due to the work of the Leicestershire Industrial History Society in restoration, the Moira Furnace is a scheduled ancient monument and a rare example.

**The Ashby Canal** was built between 1794 and 1804. It ran south for 30 miles along the 300 ft contour to join the Coventry Canal at Marston Junction near Nuneaton and it was lock-free except for the stop lock at Marston. The intention had been to link with the river Trent to the north but the canal never reached beyond the Ashby Woulds. By clever use of tramways, coal and other materials were transported to the canal. You walked on one of these as you returned to the furnace. The Ashby Canal Company was bought out by the Midland Railway in 1845 but traffic still used the canal until the 1940s when, due to subsidence problems, the northern section had to be closed and eventually filled in. Though Snarestone is now the terminus, the course of the canal can still be seen and followed in the Moira-Donisthorpe area, as you have seen. You will come across the Ashby Canal again as you walk in the Bosworth area.

**The Ashby and Nuneaton Joint Railway** opened in 1873 and its object was to take local coal to London and the South East, also serving Market Bosworth, Hinckley and Nuneaton. At its northern end it joined the Midland Railway Company's Burton to Leicester line near Overseal Sidings, now a nature reserve. Passenger traffic ended in 1931 and goods traffic in 1981. The Ashby Woulds Heritage Trail now follows part of the railway and there are plans to extend this from Donisthorpe to Oakthorpe and to Measham.

**Willesley Hall** was pulled down in 1953 and, according to Pevsner, it had 'a dramatic, probably late 17th century, facade'. The stables and majestic serpentine lake remain, as does the early 14th century church of St Thomas. Its tower is dated at 1845 and there are interesting monuments inside the church. The lovely parkland is now a golf course with a statue of Diana near the 9th hole, a left over from the past. A tramway ran from Willesley Wharf (1 mile south west of the Park, on the Ashby Canal) to Ticknall, 7 miles north near Calke Abbey, bringing in limestone.

**Ashby-de-la-Zouch** is the historic market town of the region and last century was described as 'not a manufacturing town . . . but genteel and respectable'. The name is derived from the acquisition of the manor by the Zouch family in 1160. Market rights were granted in 1219 and at one time there were four fairs a year in the town. The castle and church of St Helen, side by side, present the most distinctive feature, the latter containing very interesting monuments and the former being associated especially with Lord Hastings (c1430-83). Fictionally, there is the important link with Sir Walter Scott's 'Ivanhoe' which has given the tourist slogan for the area of Ivanhoe Country. Ashby's prominence grew when Moira failed as a spa town. The mineral water discovered during mining operations at Bath Colliery near Moira was then taken to Ashby and in 1822 the Ivanhoe Baths were built, shortly followed by the Royal Hotel in 1826. By 1846 White's Directory reported that Ashby was 'a handsome and highly salubrious market town and watering place, celebrated for its saline baths and extensive remains of its once formidable and famous baronial castle'.

Today, the main street retains an imposing aura and some fine buildings with several interesting passages, but the amount of through traffic and some of the raw edges of the town are well on the way to spoiling the historic character of the place and the enjoyment which a walker might expect to have.

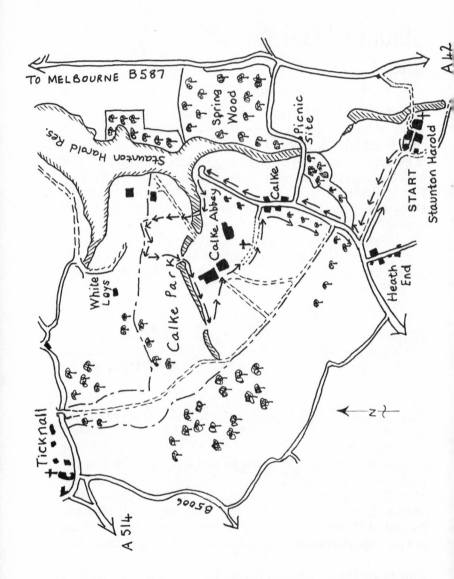

# Staunton Harold Hall and Calke Abbey

**Introduction:** This must be one of England's most outstanding walks. It begins with the idyllic scene of Staunton Harold Hall, church and lakes described by Nicholas Pevsner as 'unsurpassed in the country, certainly as far as Englishness is concerned'. The walk continues to a viewpoint overlooking the picturesque Staunton Harold Reservoir, lying partly in Leicestershire and partly in Derbyshire. It then threads its way through the beautiful landscaped grounds of Calke Abbey, skirting the famous deer park and alongside a series of attractive ponds in a deep valley, thence across open parkland to the house where 'time stood still', with its fine gardens and solitary church some distance away. Finally, you leave the park passing Calke village, now only a shrunken victim of aristocratic emparking, for the return to Staunton Harold Hall.

**Distance:** A 5 mile walk mostly in pleasant, undulating parkland, which takes about 3 hours unhurried. Allow time to appreciate Staunton Harold Hall and its environs as well as Calke Abbey. OS Landranger 128.

**Refreshments:** Coffee in Staunton Harold Hall (not Mondays) and the Stables Tearoom (not Mondays). The Nursery Tearoom is available on Mondays and at other times. There are toilets. The Saracens Head pub is conveniently located at Heath End just outside your exit gate from the hall. You see the sign as you join the main road, ½ mile from your start at the hall, to the left. Calke Abbey restaurant, shop and toilets are open from the end of March to the end of October, Saturdays to Wednesdays inclusive, 11 am to 5 pm. Open weekends 12 noon to 4 pm, November to December.

**How to get there:** Staunton Harold Hall is a few miles north of Ashby-de-la-Zouch in north west Leicestershire − 'Ivanhoe Country'. Take the A453(T) out of Ashby and turn left onto the B587 to Melbourne, Derbyshire. There are two well-signposted driveways to the hall off to the left. The first is at the turning onto the B587, the second is 1 mile further on. Staunton Harold Hall is a Cheshire Home and the nearby church is National Trust. Calke Abbey is also National Trust but there is open access to the park and grounds of both for the public. Car parking at Staunton Harold Hall without charge but please use public car parks only.

**The Walk:** Staunton Harold Hall in its setting is entrancing and you will require a strong will to leave it. However, when you are ready to move off go past the nurseries on your left with the craft workshops to your right. Follow the lane as it passes through an oak tree avenue and thence to the entrance gate at the road. Sign to Saracens Head now visible on your left. Resisting temptation, turn right and walk along the country road for ½ mile passing a closed gateway to Calke Abbey on your left.

Proceed along the road into the small village of Calke and soon you will see a pretty thatched cottage on your right and, almost opposite, the main exit from Calke Park. Go on for another ½ mile until you reach the end of the road at the Staunton Harold Reservoir picnic and car park. Here you have a wonderful view to the boathouse and dam over 1 mile away. There are tables and an information board here.

The Severn-Trent Water Authority has made this viewing point available and you will see clearly signposted their permissive pathway to the left. Follow this path alongside the reservoir. There are seats here. The path is easy to follow and you will come to wooden steps, a plank bridge and then a more solid wooden bridge where the path goes through trees and still keeps close to the reservoir. Eventually you reach a metal and concrete bridge near to a lily pond known as Little Dogkennel Pond. To your right is the reservoir. In the distance you can see a large weir.

In a short distance you come to more wooden steps and a stone wall to your right. Then you cross a farm lane with no access to left or right. The journey is now uphill with a high wire fence to your left and the stone wall to the right. Bracken is all around you and there are excellent views into Calke Abbey Deer Park to your left. If visibility is good you might be able to see one of the Trent Valley power stations to your right.

Turn sharp left, keeping the wire fence on your left. You are circuiting the deer enclosure and you can see Calke Abbey House in the distance. Again there is bracken all around.

Cross a stile which is located to the right of a farm gate. Turn sharp left round the deer enclosure going south now and you will see a big oak tree in the path. Still keeping the wire fence on your left proceed downhill. There are seats pleasantly situated in the bracken hereabouts.

Go through a small wooden gate and on to a major stone bridge between two ponds. The one on your left is called China House Pond and the one on the right is Mere Pond. There is a lovely view up the valley here.

Turn sharp right alongside the lily pond, Mere Pond, and find a finely situated seat where you can pause to contemplate the scene. The series of ponds are in an ever-deepening valley as you walk alongside them. Go through a kissing-gate up wooden steps climbing the steep valley side until you reach seats at the top.

Now carry on following the valley side with Thatch House Pond below you on your right. In about 400 yards your path begins to descend and you see a path continuing between two ponds. Do not take this but instead, turn sharp left across the open parkland and make for the cupola on the stable block of Calke Abbey. The church will be seen on the skyline to your right.

You will arrive at the stables and ticket office behind the house. You may wish to visit this unique place. Afterwards, follow the exit lane out of the park. The distance is about 1 mile and will lead you past the church which marks the original site of Calke village. There are very good views of the house from the exit road. Note the ha-ha to your left. Continue to follow the road until you reach the exit gate. Turn right on to the country lane. Walk through Calke village until you reach the main road. If time allows, you can visit Dimminsdale Nature Reserve with its nature trails just 200 yards down the road to the left. However, your route back is to go straight on from Calke village for ½ mile until you reach the sign for the Saracens Head and the entrance to Staunton Harold Hall. Return up this drive to your car.

## Historical Notes

**Staunton Harold Hall** lacks a village since this was removed in favour of sheep ranching in the 14th century. The Shirley family held the manor for over five centuries. In the early 17th century Sir Henry Shirley had a mansion built at the centre of 1,700 acres of the parish. Large deer parks were converted to farmland in 1623. The present hall was designed and built by Washington, Fifth Earl

Ferrers (1760-1778) but not quite finished at his death. This Georgian house hides earlier structures.

The formal gardens of the late 17th century were mostly swept away by the same earl who replaced them with the more 'natural' scenery we see today.

The hall narrowly escaped demolition in the 1950s, being sold in 1954. It is now a Cheshire Home.

**Holy Trinity church, Staunton Harold** (National Trust), is one of the few churches built during the Commonwealth. It was begun by Sir Robert Shirley, an ardent Royalist, in 1653 as an act of piety and defiance 'when all things sacred were throughout the Nation either demolisht or profaned'. It was well advanced by his death three years later though not fully completed until 1665. The original cushions, hangings, panelling and painted ceiling remain. There is a wrought-iron screen by Robert Bakewell. Open March to end of October, Wednesday to Sunday and Bank Holiday Mondays 11 am to 1 pm and 2 pm to 5 pm (Free-Collection box).

**The Staunton Harold Reservoir** was constructed in 1966 and is worked in association with Foremark Reservoir, 3 miles to the west. Both are pump-filled from the river Dove in Derbyshire. Water is supplied to Leicestershire and the treatment works is at the northern end, near Melbourne. There is an earth-filled dam and, close by, a picnic site, car park and adventure playground. Fishing began in 1973 and sailing in 1975. There is a boathouse at the northern end. A nature reserve which is a SSSI is in the southern section associated with Spring Wood and Dimminsdale Reserves. Readers will be interested in the wisdom of a notice to be found at the latter place: 'Please keep to the footpath. Take nothing but photographs. Leave nothing but footprints. Kill nothing but time'. One great regret is that it is not yet possible for the public to walk all the way round the reservoir. Perhaps the Severn-Trent Water Authority will introduce this one day?

**Calke Abbey** won the English Tourist Board's England for Excellence Award in 1989. Acquired by the National Trust in 1985, it was described as a secret house where time stood still. The Harpurs had lived there since 1622 and were well-known as eccentrics and recluses. Before that time the site had been settled by the Augustinians who founded a priory there in the 12th century.

Sir John Harpur (1680-1741), who had a great deal of money at his disposal, began to turn the Elizabethan courtyard house on the site into a fine Baroque mansion. By the end of the 18th century his successor, of the same name, brought the house up-to-date to fit in with the neo-Classical taste, also completing the landscaping of the park.

A later successor, Sir Vauncey Harpur Crewe (1846-1924) also displayed the family eccentricity, but this time through his passion for natural history, leading to an enormous collection which now fills the house. He also had the sensible idea of banning all motor cars from his park. His reluctance to throw anything away and to leave things as they were resulted in the house being fossilised at about the 1880s. Thus we can step back in history to Victorian times with great ease.

The park is 750 acres in extent and has been considerably re-shaped in contours, by the establishment of a chain of ponds and by tree planting, in the picturesque style. The walled gardens were built between 1772 and 1774 extending over 7 acres. There is a domed orangery dating from the 18th century, which, with the gardens, is in the process of restoration.

**St Giles Church** is 300 yards south of the house and quite close to the orchard, gardens and dairy farm. Though built in the late 16th century it was 'recased in the Gothic style' in 1827-29. Due to emparking extensions in 1769 the church, formerly near to the village of Calke, was encompassed within the park and separated from the village street which was altered. The present dairy house was originally a farmhouse on the village street. What is left of Calke village is now to be found outside the park at the Calke Gate. The house is open from the end of March to the end of October, Saturdays to Wednesdays inclusive, 12.30 pm to 5 pm. The garden is open the same days but from 11 am to 5.30 pm. The park is open every day throughout the year, no charge to pedestrians but £1 vehicle charge for non-members, refundable when a house ticket is purchased. The restaurant and shop open the same days as the house.

# Belvoir Castle and
# The Jubilee Way

**Introduction:** The far north east of Leicestershire protrudes into Lincolnshire and Nottinghamshire and it is encircled by Nottingham, Newark, Grantham and Melton Mowbray. The heart of the area is the famous Vale of Belvoir which is overlooked by a great scarp. Belvoir Castle sits in all its majesty on this ridge and below is the river Devon and the disused Grantham Canal.

This is the renowned region of pork pies, Stilton cheese, hunt cakes and world-famous hunting country. It is the most rural of rural areas and you can see a line of lovely villages located below the scarp from Long Clawson to Redmile and Bottesford. On the scarp itself another series of high level villages like Eastwell and Eaton can be found, very different in character, and in the past associated with ironstone working.

Although the Vale of Belvoir has been so deeply rural, it has been touched by industry for the 'nodding donkeys' you may see in some fields indicate that oil has been extracted for some years. Also, the vale was threatened with three major coalmines in the late 1970s but in the event only one 'Super Pit' was established at Asfordby, outside the vale, and well-landscaped into its surroundings. For years, however, coal had been mined close by in the Nottinghamshire Cotgrave field. The expansion of commuters from the cities to live in local villages has also brought change to the vale.

The Jubilee Way was opened in 1977 to mark the Queen's Silver Jubilee and extends from Melton Mowbray northwards along the scarp then down into the vale below Belvoir Castle, eventually turning east to join the Viking Way near Woolsthorpe, Lincolnshire. It is 15½ miles long. Our walk uses part of the Jubilee Way around Belvoir Castle and offers spectacular views, not only of the castle, but also over the beautiful Vale of Belvoir itself.

**Distance:** About 6½ miles of pleasant and easy walking with only one very steep hill out of Woolsthorpe and here the views back

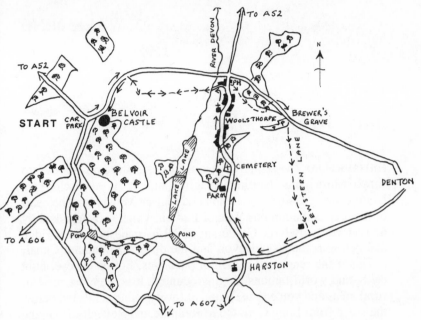

to Belvoir Castle recompense. Allow 3 hours for the walk, but you will need extra time to visit the castle. OS Landranger 130.

**Refreshments:** The Chequers inn, Woolsthorpe, and there is a village shop and post office.

**How to get there:** Follow the signs to Belvoir Castle from the A607 Melton to Grantham road and also from the A52 Grantham to Nottingham road. Turn off the A606 Nottingham to Melton road at either Nether Broughton or near Ab Kettleby for Belvoir and the vale, if you are approaching from this direction. You do not need to park in the official castle car park. Opposite, you will find a field at the corner where you can park free. It is at the start of a public footpath and the sign is there. If this is full, you will find plenty of verge-side parking available back along the road.

**The Walk:** As you leave your parking place you face the castle car park and main entrance. Go along the road on your left which is marked Jubilee Way. You will find the verges are wide enough to walk along though you may have to change from one side of the road to the other occasionally. Beware the traffic. Walk along for ¾ mile with excellent views over the vale to your left. Look for a sign, 'Jubilee Way Woolsthorpe 1 mile', on your right at

59

a clump of trees. Turn right into the field. Ahead you will see Woolsthorpe.

Walk to the left of the hedge downhill in an arable field. At a farm track and gate follow arrows pointing away from the castle so that you turn sharp left. Now keep to the left-hand side of a very large field and follow the hedge which has a number of oak trees along it. Climb a stile into the next field still keeping to the left. You see the village clearly in front of you and the path leads you to a stile and bridge over the river Devon. Ridge and furrow marking the old medieval open fields can be seen here.

Bear left past cottages into Belvoir Lane. At the main road turn left to the Chequers inn. Go up to the pub entrance but then make for the gap into the cricket field a little further on. A symbol marks this. Go across to the scoreboard. Behind it you will find a stile which you must cross into the pasture field beyond. Follow the edge of the woodland keeping it to your left side as you proceed up the steep hill. Look back for wonderful views of Belvoir Castle.

As an avenue of trees appears to your right look for a wooden gate on your left (arrows). Go over into the wood. Ignore 'Private Tipping' signs as this is the official way. Bear right. After about 200 yards cross a stile on to the main road from Belvoir to Denton. Turn right and walk for about 400 yards until you reach a lodge house on your right at the bend in the road. This is Brewer's Grave.

As the road bends you keep straight on to a wide track into woodland. You will see a blue arrow on a post marking the Viking Way. Actually this is also the Sewstern Lane, a former pre-historic trackway. You have a very pleasant walk for 1 mile along the lane, part of which runs along the Leicestershire-Lincolnshire border. Just before you reach New Cottages, near the end of the lane, you cross over a disused railway which once served the quarries hereabouts.

Turn right at the main road and walk ½ mile into Harston. You are now back in Leicestershire. As you walk along Denton Lane you will see views of Belvoir Castle on your right. In the village look for the cannon in the garden of Cannon Cottage to your right and to your left the hare weather vane.

Turn right into Woolsthorpe Lane with its very well-kept verges. There is a pleasant 1½ mile walk into the village passing on the way the sign 'Woolsthorpe by Belvoir', Castle Farm and the site of St James church with its interesting cemetery. Pause awhile to read the tombstones. Can you find Jos Buckwell, Gardener to His Grace the Duke of Rutland who died in 1827?

From the cemetery keep to the path on the left going under the bridge, past Top Cottages and into the main street of the village. When you reach Belvoir Lane turn left into it and retrace your route back to the castle. That means going across the river Devon and following the waymarked path uphill keeping to the right of each field along the line of the hedge and trees and crossing the stiles. When you come to the far corner of the very large arable field turn right at the gate and go uphill to join the main road. Turn left and follow the road until you arrive back at your car park.

## Historical Notes

**Belvoir Castle** commands a wonderful view over several counties and it is a landmark from far away. The Norman name meaning 'beautiful view' indicates the origins, since the first castle on this site was built by Robert de Todeni, standard bearer to William the Conqueror, in the 11th century. Destruction by civil wars in the 15th and 17th centuries as well as a devastating fire in 1816 left very little of the original buildings and so the present castle dates from 1800-1830.

Its outline fulfils everyone's dream of the fairy castle and, indeed, it is a favourite location for film makers, being the venue of 'Little Lord Fauntleroy' in recent years. Continually, Belvoir breaks attendance records for tourist attractions and visitors come from all over the world. There is a full programme of events throughout the summer season, one of the most exciting being medieval jousting tournaments. There are so many treasures in the castle that it is futile in a short space to attempt to name them. They range from the extraordinary, like the gigantic elk's head dug out of an Irish bog and the bugle which sounded the Charge of the Light Brigade, to the hand-painted silks of the China Room, the painted ceilings, tapestries, busts and the famous picture gallery. The castle is the home of the 17/21st Lancers Museum.

**Woolsthorpe** should not be confused with the village of the same name, also in Lincolnshire, 8 miles east near the A1 (where Sir Isaac Newton was born). This one is Woolsthorpe-by-Belvoir. It is a distinctive street village lying at the foot of the scarp and on the banks of the river Devon, but far enough off, on a river terrace, to avoid flooding. Both the Belvoir estate and hunt have influenced the village as can be seen by the hunt stables and hunt cottages at the northern end.

St James's church was south of the village in medieval times and a mound marking the foundations can be seen on your walk near the cemetery. The church was replaced in 1791 on a new site by another, itself rebuilt between 1845-47, which Pevsner describes as 'a little unexciting'. The old school takes up the style of the church and it was built in 1871.

You may not have time to get to the disued Grantham Canal, which is about a mile north of the village. The canal opened in 1797 and had 7 locks. It linked the Trent and the Witham as it meandered through the Vale of Belvoir. Stone was unloaded from the canal to build Belvoir and Harlaxton Hall, a few miles east. The Sewstern Way and the more recent Viking Way follow the Woolsthorpe section of the canal and you can see lock cottages and a wharf along this stretch.

**Brewer's Grave** is at the end of an avenue of trees where a lodge is located and where the Sewstern Way crosses the Denton-Belvoir road. I could not find any grave or memorial, perhaps you might be luckier. Apparently the name derives from a brewer at Belvoir Castle who was buried here with his donkey but at such a strategic site I suspect more devious historical reasons.

**Sewstern Lane,** otherwise known as 'The Drift', has been a drove road for centuries and before that a prehistoric trackway, certainly since Bronze Age times. It followed the high ground and linked the Trent valley with the Welland and the Fens. Its line can still be easily traced on maps as it comes south to Sewstern village then joins the Great North Road south of Stretton. For much of this length it forms a county boundary. The area you are walking through, especially near Woolsthorpe Quarries, on the Sewstern Lane, has been greatly influenced since Roman times by ironstone working and you may notice in some places the fields are lower than the roads due to removal of ironstone and subsequent restoration at a lower level.

**Harston** is at the tip of Leicestershire and near its boundary with Lincolnshire. The name means 'grey stone' which has been thought to refer to boundary stones. St Michael's church has a 14th century west tower but there is heavy restoration dated 1871-88. An Anglo-Saxon cross shaft can be found in the east wall.

# Fort Henry and the Viking Way

**Introduction:** The Viking Way is a national long distance footpath from the Humber Bridge through the Lincolnshire Wolds to the edge of the Fens, the Vale of Belvoir and finally Rutland. It ends in Oakham, just west of Rutland Water.

This walk begins at a small village, Greetham, which is on the Viking Way. Mostly, the walk covers level land with wide-ranging views over rich farmland and woodland. There is evidence of the former ironstone working in the area by way of quarries and restored fields, now below the general land surface in some parts.

Much of the walk is through the Exton estate of the Earl of Gainsborough, now run by his son, Viscount Campden, and based on Exton Hall. The estate village of Exton is lovely with thatched cottages and village green and it lies just outside the hall grounds. Nearby, overlooking the old and newer halls, is the church with nationally famous memorials inside. In the field next to the church there lies the original village, visible only by studying the undulations in the ground carefully.

Part of the estate, to the east, contains the attractive landscaped valley of the North Brook which has several lakes, woodland and a charming summer house known as Fort Henry overlooking a fine lake. A short distance to the south lie the remains of the lost village of Horn, a deserted medieval village, where each year a service is held to remember the inhabitants of long ago.

The walk returns towards Greetham mainly following the North Brook upstream. It passes through woodland, close to the Great North Road, past a working quarry, through a golf course and ends at the Wheatsheaf inn, Greetham. You will be pleasantly surprised to find such wide horizons and distant views in such a small district as Rutland. It gives a fresh and exhilarating feeling to walk across these broad acres.

**Distance:** This circular route is about 7 miles in length with easy, level walking. A few sections may be overgrown. At a brisk pace the walk should take about 3 hours but you will certainly wish

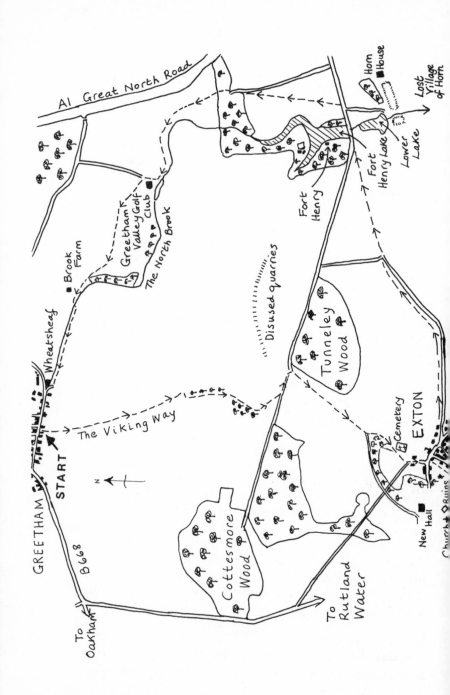

to spend time in Exton village and church, also to take refreshment at the Fox and Hounds inn on the green. Perhaps you will want to look more closely at the lost village of Horn and watch the golfers at Greetham Valley Golf Club. OS Landranger 130.

**Refreshments:** There are three pubs in Greetham, The Plough, Wheatsheaf and the Black Horse inn as well as a shop and post office. In Exton, the Fox and Hounds.

**How to get there:** From Oakham take the B668 to Cottesmore and Greetham. Alternatively, if approaching from the A1, turn off at Stretton, on to the B668 Oakham road. You will reach Greetham in 5 minutes from this direction and in about 15 minutes from the Oakham direction. Park in the main street or a side lane in Greetham. If you are patronising one of the pubs they have good car parks. The walk starts almost opposite the post office and is signposted 'The Viking Way'.

**The Walk:** Follow the sign, with a house to the left and a wall to the right, for about 100 yards. At present there are nettles along the way but I hope these will be cleared. Cross a stile and the path runs alongside a hawthorn hedge on your left. After another 100 yards you reach a stile marked with yellow arrows leading into a caravan field. Keep to the left on a gravel drive and aim for the gap and cattle grid at the nearside corner of the field.

Into a wheatfield, keeping to the track alongside the hedge, until you reach the far corner when you will see a signpost (arrows) directing you straight on into the next field through a large gap in the hedge. You may notice that the fields are very stony and if you pick up a stone you will find it to be oolitic limestone which looks like lots of cod roe cemented together. The landscape is flat and fertile with arable fields all around, punctuated now and then by woodland.

Again, keep straight on into the next field with a high hedge and solitary ash tree to your right. Follow the hedge line to a distant ash tree at the far corner of the field.

Here, at a stile and post (yellow arrows) cross a footbridge into a wheatfield. Turn sharp right then, after 50 yards, turn left on to a gravel farm track which goes alongside a row of trees on your left.

Follow the track as it skirts a small wood when old quarries and parkland come into view. As the track bends left take the small wooden gate in front of you (arrows). Cross a footbridge and then walk diagonally across the field to the far left side where you will find a stile (arrows). Here you rejoin the white farm track. Follow it as it bears left with a fence on your left and wheatfield on your right. Now turn right at the Viking Way post on to a metalled road. The wood nearby is Tunneley Wood.

Walk along this road for about ½ mile when you come to a fork. Go to the left, keeping a wood on your right-hand side. A marker shows the way. Carry on past the cemetery over cattle grids into Exton village via an estate farmyard which leads you into West End. Exton estates workshops are here too.

Proceed into the village High Street, then to the green. Here you may wish to pause at the Fox and Hounds for refreshment. Next, continue down from the green until you see a signpost on your left for the parish church. Go into the lane leading to the church noting, eventually, on your left the humps and bumps of the old village, and on your right, the old hall (burnt down in 1810) and, behind, the new hall.

When you have finished looking inside the church go back down the lane to the main road. Turn left and return to the green. Cross the green to the far corner and go onto Stamford Road. As soon as you reach this road you will see, almost opposite you, New Field Road. Sycamore trees mark the road. Go into this road and walk between the bungalows until you reach a sign on a gate about Exton estates. Although unauthorised traffic may not use this road it is a right of way for walkers and you can proceed along it. The road is well surfaced and runs in an avenue of trees. In the distance you will see Ketton Cement Works to the right, Exton church behind you and, soon, A1 traffic in the distance. Nearby is the ridge and furrow of the old village fields of medieval times.

After ½ mile the road bears left. Carry on for another ½ mile until you reach another road crossing yours. Do not go left or right but straight on into the field opposite you where a well-marked grass lane leads you to the surfaced road between Fort Henry Lake and the Lower Lake.

Now you may wish to spend a little time observing this magnificent scene and, if you wish, you can take the lane to the site of the lost village of Horn on the far side of the Lower Lake.

When you are ready, carry on along the road uphill, until, on your right, you see a metalled track joining. Almost opposite here cross the large field on your left and make for the distant corner, diagonally, aiming for the end of the woods (Horn Lane Spinney). If this field route is impassable due to crops you may take a surfaced track which runs through the field and can be reached by walking a further 250 yards up the main road.

As you follow the track through the woods for about 150 yards, you come to a T junction. Turn right for 15 yards only and look for two white gateposts. Then turn left past these and through a gap in the trees here to a white stone stile in 100 yards at the edge of the wood. This may be the roughest part of the walk!

Cross the stile into the field and make for a stone ruin in the middle of the field, which may have been a windmill, following a stunted hedge line. With a quarry ahead of you, walk towards the wooden gate at the far side of the field. Go through this, crossing the small field to reach another wooden gate opposite. The North Brook is to your left.

Go through the gate into a small lane. Directly opposite you will find another gate. When you have passed through this go for about 200 yards and climb over another wooden gate on your left. Keep to the hedge line and fence on your left until it leads you to a sign (arrows) near a farm track. Cross a stile into the field. You have now reached Greetham Valley Golf Course. Bear left following the hedge line to a marked post (arrows) under an ash tree. Carry on a stone track for 100 yards to the next marker. The golf range is to your right. In front you will see a pool and stream which are part of the course.

Turn right at the marker and go uphill with the club-house on your left. Look for another marker post at the edge of the entry road to the golf club. Opposite there is a sign to the par 3 course. Turn left into a wide track past a marker post near the hedge. Keep to this track as it bears left for 300 yards, eventually to follow a hedge line.

At the end of the track a marker post indicates a gap in the hedge. Go through the gap and turn sharp right alongside another hedge. Keep this on your right as it continues towards the edge of a spinney about 400 yards away.

Just before you reach the spinney you come to a stile in the hedge. This has a marker post on it. In the distance you can see the spire of Greetham church and also the village. Cross the stile and make for the chimney of Brook Farm which you can see diagonally across the field. When you reach the hedge at the far side of the field you will see a stile which you can cross into a pasture field. If there is a growing crop in the field you have just crossed then you can alternatively go via the corner of the field close to the spinney to avoid trampling the crop.

Once in the pasture field, walk downhill to the stream, mid-way along its course. Walk alongside the stream to the corner of the field where you will find a stile very close to the stream. Cross over the stile and walk upstream for 100 yards to a telegraph pole. This marks the location of a plank over the stream. Cross the plank and follow the hedge line keeping it on your right-hand side. There is some rough ground at the edge of the fields here but in summer there are many lovely poppies acting as a colourful border. Continue for just less than ½ mile until you enter Wheatsheaf Lane, next to the happy relief to be obtained at the delightful Wheatsheaf inn. You have now arrived back in Greetham.

## Historical Notes

**Greetham** is situated just over 1 mile from the Great North Road and the pre-historic Sewstern Way is even closer. Now the Viking Way runs through the village and the NATO air base at Cottesmore is 1 mile to the north west. Rutland Water is about 4 miles to the south. Thus, both in the past and present, Greetham has been close to communications and activities. It has also been the centre of quarrying for building stone and ironstone as the many disused quarries around show and the village houses indicate.

North Brook runs through the village and, indeed, the fountain is a reminder of the importance of water: –

> 'All ye who hither come to drink,
> Rest not your thoughts below,
> Remember Jacob's Well and think
> Whence living waters flow'

Thus speaks the fountain. This was a well-watered place since once there were at least four public pumps, and there is a Pond Lane, but the pond was filled in 60 years ago. Eventually North Brook flows to Fort Henry then past the lost village of Horn and eventually to Empingham where it joins the river Gwash below Rutland Water dam.

Greetham is an ancient site. Romano-British finds have been made here and at Thistleton, a little to the north. Also, the nucleus of -ham name endings round this area (Greetham, Empingham,

Clipsham, Bytham and Witham) suggest an important Saxon settlement just off the old Roman road. The original manor house and some village buildings seem to have been located to the north west of the church where there were earthworks, now built over. As you walk down Sheepdyke Lane where the old sheep wash used to be, you come to St Mary's with its tall broach spire and decorated west tower. The chancel is 13th century, perhaps the rebuilding of the Norman church. In 1897 considerable restoration was required as the church was reported to be 'in a ruinous condition'. Inside there are many old carvings and figures built into the walls.

In Great Lane you will find the former stonemason's workshop of the Halliday family which is like a stonemason's scrapbook since it has historic samples of stonework built into its walls.

Once, Greetham belonged to the Earls of Warwick, until the 15th century. Later it passed to the Finch family of Burley-on-the-Hill and many estate records show the daily business and disputes related to the village. The enclosure was early for Rutland, in 1763, and an interesting, unusual system of cottage smallholdings subsequently developed so that in 1901 there were 43 smallholders with parcels of land ranging from 5 to 80 acres.

**Exton Village** is one of the prettiest in Rutland. It lies outside the great hall of the Noels, Haringtons and now the Earl of Gainsborough and Viscount Campden. It is an estate village but once you leave the attractive centre there are a few modern raw edges. Walk down High Street, West End and Pudding Bag Lane to see thatched cottages, spacious estate farms and lovely trees. The film 'Little Lord Fauntleroy' featured the village street and the church in its locations. There are many cottages dating from the 18th century; for example, the farmhouse in Top Street (1701) as well as estate cottages of the 19th century. Once, the village lay to the south of the church and signs of this can be seen in the earthworks in the pasture field. It seems that when the old hall burnt down in 1810, part of the village had to be removed to accommodate the new hall which was further north. However, this cannot account for the wholesale change of site which must have taken place earlier, in medieval times.

**Exton Hall and Park** dominate the village though the hall is secluded from it. The attractive landscaped park around the hall has ornamental lakes and fine trees and the gates and lodges at the end of drives set it all off marvellously. But the Great Park was east of the village and extended to the Great North Road. Large ornamental lakes were constructed here also, notably at Fort Henry, a pretty Gothic summerhouse 1785-90, Horn and Cuckoo Farm, mostly associated with the North Brook. This was a post-medieval park and the estate still occupies much of the same area today.

In the 12th century, King David of Scotland, and later Robert de Brus, held lands in Exton. Sir James Harington built the old hall (burnt down in 1810) in the reign of Elizabeth I and 'one of the glories of Exton church' is the monument to Sir James and his wife there. The new hall was mostly built in the 1850s but is rarely open to the public. However, it can be seen from the rear of the churchyard, beyond the ruins of the old hall.

**St Peter and St Paul, Exton,** was hailed by Pevsner: 'There are no churches in Rutland and few in England in which English sculpture from the 16th to the 18th centuries can be studied so profitably and enjoyed so much as at Exton'. He notes that there are nine important monuments, several outstanding. Some of the work is by Grinling Gibbons and Nollekins. Additionally, there are banners and funerary helmets of the Noels and Haringtons.

The 14th century spire, of a somewhat unusual outline, was struck by lightning in 1843 which left it in such a state that both tower and spire had to be virtually rebuilt. Much of the rest of the church was also extensively restored between 1852-54. Hoskins loved Exton so much that he said 'it should be a climax for the day'.

**Horn** is a deserted medieval village site south of Fort Henry and on the Exton estate. Horn House is an existing dwelling to the east of the village. North Brook flows through the site and the lower lake, popular with fishermen, is at the site. A hollow way comes downhill from Horn House and is flanked by foundations. Across the stream there is a large rectangular moat with an associated enclosure and building foundations. Horn was mentioned in the Domesday Book (1086) but was declared of little value by 1376 and in 1384 a reference states 'the whole village was then wasted and destroyed'. Later it was included in Exton Park and a fine wall crosses the site. Horn Mill, ½ mile south of the site was occupied by Thomas Wiles in 1665 (Hearth Tax Returns) and in recent times there was a trout hatchery at Horn Mill.

# Clipsham and Pickworth

**Introduction:** For centuries the Great North Road, now the A1, has cut Rutland in two. Oakham, the county town, was the hub of activities west of the road. It has been easy to forget the area to the east. Here, the villages of Clipsham, Stretton, Pickworth, Essendine, Ryhall, Belmesthorpe and Casterton gravitate more towards Stamford in Lincolnshire, never more than 12 miles away.

This isolated bastion of Rutland was a salient into Lincolnshire. It was a frontier region and, indeed, near to Pickworth, the road into that county is called the Lincolnshire Gate. The Fens begin only a few miles to the east and Hereward the Wake's town of Bourne lies no more than 6 miles away from the Rutland border.

Since 1974, when Rutland became a District of Leicestershire, this area is even more remote from its present central city, as Leicester is more than 30 miles distant. On your walk you may feel some of this isolation. There are few farms between the villages, much woodland, some very extensive, and fine stone buildings as well as field walls. The area is different.

Old and working quarries punctuate the skyline. There were famous stone quarries at Clipsham and not far away at Holywell, Barnack and Ketton which provided stone for cathedrals such as Ely and Peterborough, Oxford colleges, churches, country houses and the rebuilt House of Commons. You can see some of these quarries on your walk.

This is also John Clare country and you might well carry a copy of his poetry with you as you visit his haunts, such as the restored lime kiln at Pickworth where he worked. At this village, too, there is a mysterious arch standing alone in a field. A few miles to the south west a battle in the Wars of the Roses was fought in 1470 at Losecoat Field. Near to Clipsham village is the famous 200 year old Yew Tree Avenue, once part of the Clipsham Hall estate. History is all around in this very atmospheric area.

**Distance:** A rectangular circuit of 5 miles with reasonable field-walking and woodland paths, some of which may be muddy. Allow

71

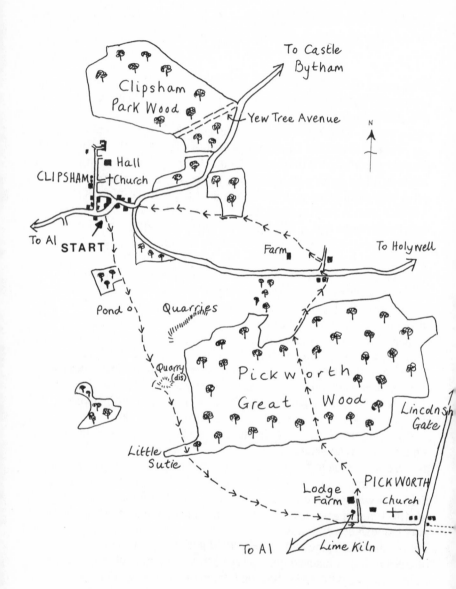

3 hours as you will want to pause a while at Pickworth. OS Landranger 130.

**Refreshments:** The excellent Olive Branch pub is at the start and end of your walk but I suggest rationing yourselves to one visit only as the real ale is powerful!

**How to get there:** Leave the A1 at Stretton and follow signposted route to Clipsham village about 1½ miles away. If approaching from the Grantham-Stamford road B1176 turn off at Little Bytham or Careby for Clipsham. The walk starts opposite the Olive Branch car park and is marked by a bridleway sign. If you are patronising the pub you may park there, but contact the landlord. Otherwise, you can find a quiet park near the church. If you don't mind an extra mile adding to your walk you can park at the Yew Tree Avenue, outside the village on the Clipsham to Bytham road, which has picnic tables and a most pleasant situation. You would then walk into the village to start your walk proper.

**The Walk:** The bridle path sign is opposite the Olive Branch car park. Walk between trees to an iron gate a short distance in front of you. An arrow indicates a hunting gate in the fence ahead. Go through the gate into a large pasture field then aim for the left corner of the woodland in front.

Go through the iron gate here into an arable field and keep to the edge of the wood as you walk uphill. Carry on past the ruins of Clipsham Lodge on your right. Cross the field to the clump of trees in front of you at the far side. Make for a gap between the trees and here you will find a pond on your right.

Follow the farm track as it bears left and runs at the side of a hedge. With the hedge on your left you will come to an isolated ash tree. Continue to follow the hedge line and you will pass signs reading 'Danger Deep Quarry'. As you reach the corner of the field you will get an excellent view into the working quarry and see fine limestone sections. Note the vast area of arable land around plus extensive woodland.

Follow the hedge line into the next field until you come to a clump of trees hiding a disused quarry. An arrow on a post directs you right and around the trees, turning left into a farm track. Bear right round the old quarry. As the track goes into the quarry you must turn right and go round the outside edge, walking in the field.

Now you must be very careful. Look across to the woodland

73

on the far side of the very large field – Little Sutie Wood. Aiming for the corner of the wood, where it bends at right angles, walk across the field towards it. The farmer should have left a path between the crop for you. If so it will be easy. You arrive at a gap in the wood where you can see a woodland path. You may have to search for it. Go along it and it will lead you to a hunting gate at the far side of the wood.

Cross the arable field diagonally left, again the farmer should have made a visible pathway through any growing crop, to a large iron gate. Go on to a farm track into the next field. You will pass several oak trees to your left and Pickworth comes into view ahead.

After ½ mile you reach the main road to Pickworth. Turn left along it passing the village road sign. A few yards further on the left you see the restored lime kiln where John Clare worked. Ponder awhile here and read his 'Eternity of Nature'. Consider that on this very site he 'hunted curious flowers in rapture & mutterd thoughts in their praise'.

Back to the main road into the village but you turn left at the bridle path sign and walk through Lodge Farm yard. You should go to look at the village before you do this and perhaps you have noticed the earthworks in the field as you came to the bridle path sign? After passing through the farmyard go to the iron gates in front of you and turn sharp left following the track round the field. Go all the way round until you reach an open red iron gate. You have arrived at Pickworth Great Wood. Carry straight on along the woodland track. When you come to a main track turn right. Continue along this track as you eventually see houses come into view on your left. Proceed downhill with woodland on your right. Go through double iron gates and follow the track to the main road, passing onto it via wooden gates next to a house.

Turn left at the main road and then, after only a few yards, right into a track which has a wood on its left and a school-like building (now a house) on its right. In a short distance take the left turn to a farm (New Quarry Farm). Do not go up to the farm, but veer to the right of the drive making for the far corner of the field. Go through the wood gate here into a pasture field keeping to the hedge on your right.

Continue into the next field via a gap in the hedge and through an iron gate onto a farm track. Cross this and continue to follow the hedge in front of you walking on its left side. You reach a fine new wooden gate into the next field. Go through and follow the tree line and wire fence keeping to the left until you reach a gap into the next field. Again, follow the line of trees and you come to a broken gate and gap leading into a very large arable field. You must now cross this field diagonally making for houses in the distance, noting a double-gabled house in particular. Keep also to the left of a large tree in the middle of the field. You should arrive at the village signpost on the main road. Carry straight on now and round the corner to the left for the Olive Branch, and the end of the walk.

## Historical Notes

**Clipsham** is one of the best Rutland villages with complete harmony visually in its limestone buildings. It is the best possible advert for the famous Clipsham Stone, once produced locally in great abundance. The local quarries were worked from as early as the 13th century, probably even earlier, and they are part of the great stone belt of England with Ancaster, Barnack, Holywell and Ketton building stone nearby. Of course, many of the quarries are now disused. Roman iron working was discovered at Clipsham and a substantial building of the 2nd and 4th centuries located here, making this an important early industrial area.

A map of the lordship dated 1687 shows that the village layout was different from today. Amongst other differences was the absence of New Road, which was not built until the 19th century by the squire. There are many good 17th century houses such as Manor and Church Farms. Considerable earthworks exist between the present village and the church.

The hall and its parkland create space close to the village. The church of St Mary is next to the hall with a lovely stonewall lane leading to it. The striking hall is mainly 18th century but a datestone of 1582 shows earlier sections. Its roofscape is fascinating. Note the unusual yew hedge separating the church and hall. At one time the manor belonged to the Zouche family of Harringworth and later came into the possession of Ezekial Johnson, grandson of Archdeacon Robert Johnson, founder of Oakham and Uppingham schools in 1584. There had been a connection between Clipsham and Oakham in so far as the former, despite its distance away from the latter, was nevertheless in the Soke of Oakham. Now the hall is occupied by the Davenport-Handley family with Cheshire links to Bramhall Hall.

St Mary's church has a memorable spire of the 13th-14th centuries of unusual design. The interior is earlier with a Norman arcade and font. There was remodelling in the 14th century when the aisles were widened and a major restoration in 1858 with, it is thought, the raising of the roof and the insertion of the east window as well as the rebuilding of the north wall of the north aisle. There are many interesting faces carved around the church and the heraldic glass in the east window came from Pickworth.

Clipsham's landscape has many differences from the rest of Rutland, mainly due to the limestone geology. There are intermittent streams, swallow holes and shake holes, dry valleys and a profusion of quarries, now mainly disused. Additionally, there is a much greater expanse of woodland, indeed the village is virtually surrounded by Pickworth Great Wood, Osbonall Wood, Stretton Wood, Addah Wood, Little Haw Wood and Clipsham Park Wood. Beyond all these lie Morkery Wood and Greetham Wood Near and Far.

**Clipsham Yew Tree Avenue** leads through Clipsham Park Wood, now owned by the Forestry Commission. It was once part of the Clipsham Hall estate. The avenue is 700 yards long from the car park and picnic area on the Bytham road out of Clipsham, extending in the direction of the hall. The 200 years old yews were first cut into shapes by Amos Alexander in 1870 and the tradition has continued. Spitfires, battleships, ballerinas, a fox and hounds, animals, initials, local characters and even 'diddy-men' have been cut out of the trees but, lately, the clippers have become less ambitious or less skilled.

**Clipsham Quarry** lies south east of the village and you have a fine view of it along your walk. It is one of the few remaining quarries into this famous stone and now the purpose is often for use as lime or road metal and infill. Here you can see fine sections of the Upper Estuarine Series, Upper and Lower Lincolnshire Limestone.

**Pickworth** is now a much shrunken village with Lodge Park Farm, Manor Farm and a few cottages at the crossroads where The Drift begins. Once it was larger as the earthworks near the lime kilns and behind Manor Farm show. The present church dates from the 1820s and must be considered tomb-like and ugly. The earlier church was said to have been destroyed at the Battle of Losecoat Field in 1470 though a map of 1710 shows a church symbol slightly west of the present church. The ruined tower and spire were taken down between 1728-31 though, apparently it had been 'a very fine steeple, seen all round the country'. All that remains of the old church is the arch in the field.

**John Clare (1793-1864),** the so-called 'Peasant Poet', was born in Helpston, a few miles east of Stamford, on the edge of the Fens. He came to Rutland in 1817 to work as a lime-burner at Great Casterton and he also worked at Pickworth at the lime kilns, now restored, and on your walk. He enjoyed the scenic qualities and peace of the district as shown in some of his poems. He was entranced by Pickworth, calling it 'a place of other days'. He mentions many local features in his 'Autobiography, Elegy on the Ruins of Pickworth, Rutlandshire, Hastily Composed', and 'Written with a Pencil on the Spot'. He stayed in the area until 1819 when he met Patty (Martha) Turner whom he married on 20th March, 1820, at Great Casterton church. Clare is one of our leading poets of natural history and rural life and his detailed observations are of outstanding value, interest and inspiration.

**The Battle of Losecoat Field** in 1470 took place near Pickworth Plain in the vicinity of the Great North Road near a wood subsequently named Bloody Oaks. It is also called the Battle of Empingham, though that village is 2 miles further away and, in fact, Horn and Hardwick were nearer. Early descriptions place the battle 'in a felde called Hornefelde'. Now both Horn and Hardwick are deserted villages, Pickworth is a shrunken village and another nearby village named Woolfox is no more. How far the battle led to these villages being destroyed may never be known.

Lincolnshire rebels, hoping to join up with the Earl of Warwick, moved towards Leicestershire but were intercepted by Edward IV coming up the Great North Road from Stamford. A fierce encounter followed in which one discharge of Edward's artillery scattered the rebels who, to escape more speedily and avoid recognition, cast aside their coats, thus giving the battle its popular name.

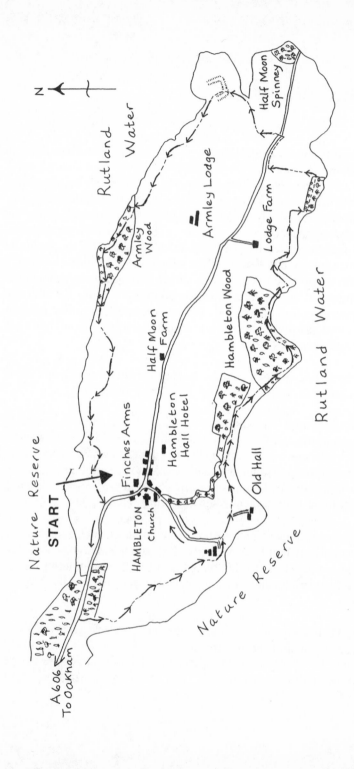

# Rutland Water

**Introduction:** Rutland Water is the largest man-made lake in England. It is the size of Windermere in the Lake District but it is a relatively new feature in Rutland's landscape, being opened in 1976. It would take a whole day to walk around Rutland Water completely but the Hambleton Peninsula, which protrudes into the horseshoe-shaped reservoir, gives an excellent view of all parts. The peninsula walk follows permitted footpaths round the peninsula created by Anglian Water for the enjoyment of visitors and to give access to fishermen. The route is varied, passing through woodland, pasture and arable land with the southern section flat and the northern section undulating. Please note that dogs must be kept on a lead. Swimming is not allowed. Cyclists and some motorists can use the tracks and beware starting fires!

**Distance:** About 5 miles in a circular route. The walk takes about 2½ hours as a leisurely stroll. OS Landranger 141.

**Refreshments:** The village of Hambleton occupies the centre of the peninsula and here the Finches Arms has excellent bar snacks and meals in a restaurant. There is a lovely terrace overlooking the north shore of Rutland Water. Spacious car parking is available. For gourmets with more time available there is the exclusive Hambleton Hall hotel further down the village road.

**How to get there:** Hambleton is about 2 miles from Oakham, once the county town of Rutland. Leave Oakham via the A606 Stamford Road and turn right to Hambleton about 1 mile out of town. There is parking in the village and, for intended customers, at the Finches Arms.

**The Walk:** Start in the village with the church on your right and proceed downhill. Follow the narrow lane to the shore of Rutland Water. As you descend there are splendid views over the nature reserve and towards Lax Hill. You reach an information board which has a map of Rutland Water for you to consult. Cross over a cattle grid and opposite, about ½ mile away, is the fine Jacobean Old Hall, jutting out into Rutland Water. Do not go into the private road leading to the old hall. Instead, turn left and follow the gravel path. This distinctive surface is found all along the route and will keep you on the right path.

Before moving off, look back westwards at fine views over the nature reserve. Bird watchers will find much to interest them here and should bring a spotter's guide with them.

Continue, with woodland to your left and shoreline to your right, round a bay, looking back towards the old hall and Lax Hill, especially beautiful at sunset. Cross a cattle grid and enter Hambleton Wood. There are side paths through to the waterline at various points.

Emerging from the wood, cross another cattle grid and walk through grassland with excellent views towards Rutland Sailing Club on the south shore and Edith Weston church beyond. Go through a small wood and then turn at right angles to the left between arable fields. Pause a while at the gate near the corner for a good view of Normanton Tower and behind, Normanton Park Hotel − all that remains of the great mansion of Lord Ancaster. You also have a nearer view of Rutland Sailing Club and, in the distance, a large aerial denoting the site of RAF North Luffenham.

The path takes a couple of sharp right-angled bends again to right and left. You cross the former road from Hambleton to Normanton which is now a dead-end. If you have time, go down to the end of this road to see how it disappears into the water near Half Moon Spinney. Can you see it re-emerge at the far side?

Return to your route, turn right and continue north over a cattle grid. Look for signs of a moated site near to a fisherman's car park. There are now excellent views towards the dam (¾ mile long). Can you see Empingham church peeping over the top? You will also see a huge tower sticking out of the water, most of it below water level. This is the limnological tower used to examine water quality.

Follow the path through grassland as it turns along the north shore of the peninsula. Did you hear and see the spring on your left? There are good views of the well-landscaped picnic park at Whitwell, across the water. Look for the 'Rutland Belle' berthed alongside here. You can go for cruises on Rutland Water from Whitwell. It is also a centre for fishing, day sailing, cycling and nature trails.

Enter Armley Wood. The path emerges into grassland with spectacular views of Burley-on-the-Hill House, improving all the time as you proceed westwards. To the right, across the water, note another tower above water level — the secondary draw off tower — which can drain this part of the reservoir if necessary. Barnsdale Country Club and, nearby, Barnsdale picnic park, are also visible.

The path now undulates and crosses several cattle grids. Keep looking for views towards Oakham and the Vale of Catmose, over the nature reserve and again to Burley-on-the-Hill. Your path reaches the main road where there is another cattle grid and information board. Go downhill, away from the village, for ½ mile. Excellent views continue and the lagoons of the nature reserve are now visible. Turn left down a gravel path where you see 'No Swimming' signs, through young woodland. You are now very close to the nature reserve which is to your right. Views of Hambleton village church are to your left with good ridge and furrow on the slopes.

Cross a cattle grid through sheep pasture on the edge of Rutland Water. Again, good views to Lax Hill. As you approach, there are some buildings — this is all that remains of Middle Hambleton. The construction of the reservoir resulted in the disappearance of Lower Hambleton and part of Middle Hambleton.

In a short distance you reach the information board which you consulted at the start of your walk. Turn left and return uphill to Hambleton.

### Historical Notes

**Hambleton:** Before 1976 this was a normal 'inland' village, afterwards it was almost situated on an island in Rutland Water. It is linked to the 'mainland' by a low, narrow isthmus. Once there were three Hambletons but the reservoir caused the lower and middle villages to vanish and shrink respectively leaving the upper village on its prominent hill top. At Domesday Hambleton and its associated settlements had a population of 750 with three priests, three churches, a mill and 45 ploughs. Later there was a weekly market and annual fair. Earlier, the village belonged to the Queens of Mercia and may well have been a royal centre.

The 12th century church of St Andrew has a characteristic stumpy broach spire and next to it is a 16th century Priest's House.

**Rutland Water:** Has a surface area of more than 3,000 acres and covers 3% of the old county of Rutland. Royal Assent for the scheme was given in 1970. There was a need for water to supply domestic and industrial demand in surrounding towns which were expanding, such as Peterborough, Corby and Northampton. The reservoir was to be supplied by pumping water from the rivers Welland and Nene to the south via tunnels north into the horseshoe-shaped valleys of Rutland.

Leisure developments at Rutland Water are now as important as water supply. There are three picnic parks on the north shore at Barnsdale, Whitwell and Syke's Lane and another on the south shore at Normanton. Additionally, there is a visitors' centre at Lyndon on the south shore where the public can follow a nature trail and observe wildlife from hides nearby. A few miles away at Egleton there is another area of nature reserve for permit holders. Cruises are available from Whitwell which is also the centre for fishing and day sailing. Here, too, cycles can be hired, as they can at Normanton. There are miles of cycle tracks around the reservoir. The tourist information office is located at Syke's Lane.

**Hambleton Old Hall:** 'Newly erected' in 1611 this Jacobean house retains many fine features and is one of the few landmarks along the shores of Rutland Water. It was purchased by the Barker family in 1634 who later moved to Lyndon Hall, their chief mansion. One of the most famous of the family was Squire Thomas Barker (1733-1809) who kept weather records and nature notes for more than 60 years, now published in 'Weather Journals of a Rutland Squire' (Rutland Record Society, 1988). He was the brother-in-law of Gilbert White. A recent episode of 'Dr Who' was filmed at the old hall. Rutland Water and its environs have been a favourite location for film makers, Chekov's 'The Seagull' being set on the shoreline and several episodes of 'Upstairs, Downstairs' at Burley-on-the-Hill.

**Normanton Tower:** This was once the church of St Matthew but, as a result of the reservoir construction, it was deconsecrated. In order to protect it and leave it as a prominent landmark, the Normanton Tower Trust with Anglian Water, filled the church to window level with limestone, rubble and concrete. A bank and causeway were then built giving protection and access. A new door was made at the east end. The church was once the mausoleum for the Heathcote and Ancaster families and remains had to be removed for burial elsewhere. Now Normanton Tower is a water museum which the public can visit.

The village of Normanton was close by the church but about 1764 the villagers were removed to Empingham and the village left deserted due to the emparking activities of the Heathcotes. The church remained in solitary isolation and eventually it was rebuilt in the style of a London church, St John's, Smith Square, Westminster. This appears very incongruous in its rural environment.

Until 1925, Normanton Hall stood near the church but then it was sold and demolished. One outstanding remnant is Normanton Park hotel, once the stable block, now beautifully restored to different uses. The full story of Normanton is told in a booklet 'Normanton Tower: Rutland Water' available on site.

**Edith Weston:** This charming village is named after Queen Edith, wife of Edward the Confessor, to whom it belonged as part of her dowry in the mid 11th century, but it was taken over by William the Conqueror in 1075. There are large estates of married quarters near the village belonging to RAF North Luffenham. The Rutland Sailing Club is nearby and there is a famous Domesday Oak. In the church there is a monument to Sir Gilbert Heathcote, founder of the Bank of England.

**Burley-on-the-Hill House:** This is one of the finest houses in England and was once called 'the palace on the hill'. It is located on a site with great historical continuity. The Duke of Buckingham owned a house there which was destroyed in the Civil War. Daniel Finch, 2nd Earl of Nottingham, bought the property and, between 1694 and 1708, built the splendid house we see today. The cost was about £30,000. The church of Holy Cross, now redundant, stands close to the house.

The construction of Rutland Water has enhanced the south face of Burley and the grounds, laid out by Humphrey Repton, still present many attractive features. But the real surprise is on the north face where curving colonnades embrace a great cour d'honneur supposedly second only in size to the forecourt of St Peter's, Rome.

Burley, once the home of Oakham's lord of the manor, has been sold and will become a country house hotel but its architecture and history will be safeguarded. The full story of Burley is in 'Heritage on the Hill' (Rutland Record Society, 1990).

# Lost Village Ramble

**Introduction:** Between Oakham and Uppingham in Rutland there are a series of ridges and valleys. Small streams run west to east and when the sun shines the red soils of Rutland are highlighted in the arable fields, particularly on the ridge tops.

On the Martinsthorpe ridge there are wonderful views towards Rutland Water and Burley House on the skyline. All around, as you look, you will see church spires and villages within a few miles but mostly you will feel a sense of space and isolation here. This is enhanced by a solitary building in a field which is all that remains of the former village of Martinsthorpe. As you inspect the ground you will see the characteristic shapes that give clues to the former houses, roads and moated manor house.

This walk will take you into the land of the lost. You will find villages fossilised in the landscape if you know where to look. Apart from Martinsthorpe you will also need to look for Gunthorpe lost village which is close to Gunthorpe Hall on the opposite side of the valley. In fact, if you could go down the Gwash valley which divides the former villages, you would find several more lost villages, one drowned by the creation of Rutland Water, others, like Normanton, lost due to the emparking activities of a great lord in the 18th century.

Halfway round the walk you will find the remarkable village of Brooke with its unique church, growing, it seems from the ground, more like a natural feature than a man-made one. Once there was a flourishing priory nearby and there are many earthworks to show how the landscape changed due to the priory. Also, the village was much bigger. The version you see now is a shrunken one.

**Distance:** This is an easy and very pleasant 5 mile ramble along the Martinsthorpe ridge to Brooke returning via the Gunthorpe ridge with the river Gwash in the valley below. This river runs into Rutland Water. Allow a comfortable 3 hours.

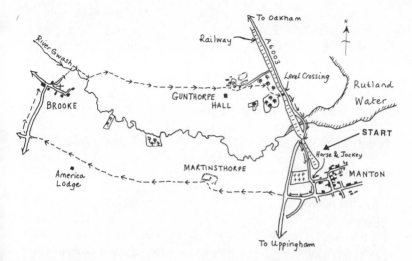

**Refreshments:** The walk begins near the Horse and Jockey pub where parking is available on the approach road. Since the walk also ends here you can refresh yourself again if you wish, perhaps on a fine day, at the tables outside the pub. OS Landranger 141.

**How to get there:** From Oakham take the A6003 to Uppingham but turn left at the Manton sign 3 miles out of Oakham. Then turn first left down a lane to the Horse and Jockey. Alternatively, if approaching from the A47 and Uppingham go along the A6003 through Preston and then, just over 1 mile further on, turn right at the Manton sign. Take first left down to the Horse and Jockey. Parking is possible on the approach to the pub.

**The Walk:** Walk back to the A6003. Opposite you there is a farm track on the far side of the dual carriageway. Cross the road very carefully into this track. The path is very clear between hedges and then across a field. Go through a large gate and follow the double line of hawthorns to your left. Cross the field to a gate in the stone wall of the next field.

As you enter this field you will see an isolated and empty building surrounded by undulations in the ground. This is the deserted village of Martinsthorpe. Pass the building and make for the pylon a short distance away. You will reach a concrete track leading to a cattle grid. Carry on along until you pass a track on the left to America Lodge. For the next ½ mile the track has a good surface.

You now reach the road between Brooke and Ridlington. Turn right to Brooke walking downhill for ½ mile until you arrive at Brooke. Turn right and pass the church on your right, bearing left down a farm track passing houses and a farm on your left. Go over a bridge which crosses the river Gwash and then turn sharp right into a grass track with hedges on both sides. This is a bridleway and should be signposted.

You come to a gate and can enter a field walking to the left side uphill. At the top follow alongside another hedge, keeping it to your left, until you reach a large gap into the next field. Go through the gap and keep to the left of the hedge. Soon you will come to a concrete track leading uphill over a cattle grid. As the track bears left you must go straight on with a wood on your right to a large wooden gate.

You pass a house and stables on your left and reach a drive. Turn right and then sharp left on the drive past a horse chestnut tree in the middle of a triangular patch and also behind Gunthorpe Hall. Soon you pass a sign and come to a double iron gate to your right. Go through and follow a grass track past cottages on your left. Ahead, a wood curves round the field. Walk all the way round the edge of the wood to the far corner.

Here you will have to look carefully for a partially obscured path through the wood. This leads into a small field and you will see a level crossing over a railway for the use of walkers. Look very cautiously in both directions before crossing and in a few yards you are on the A6003. Cross over with great care to the wide verge on the far side. Walk along to the right and in three minutes you will reach signs showing Rutland Water cycle circuit. Follow this track under the railway bridge then turn left at a small gate on to the old road which was superseded by the later by-pass. In 500 yards of uphill walking you will arrive at the Horse and Jockey and your parking place.

## Historical Notes

**Martinsthorpe** is a deserted village. Only one building remains on the site amidst what appears to be a jumble of earthworks. The location is impressive, on the north-facing slope of a ridge with views all around. The settlement was first mentioned in 1199 and in 1327 there were 14 householders — a village population of about 70. The Fielding family became the Earls of Denbigh in 1622 and built a mansion at Martinsthorpe which was demolished in 1755, except the chapel, and the stables were turned into a house. For many years this was a shepherd's house but it is now dilapidated. The last person to be born in this house was a Mrs Spink who died in March, 1978. Parts of the old chapel could be seen in 1908 but now only a small mound marks its site.

The plan or layout of the former village can be seen on the ground. Near the chapel mound another mound represents the mansion, Martinsthorpe House, and to the south there are traces of the gardens and terraces. North of the existing building is a large square enclosure with ditches which is believed to have been the old manor house of medieval times. The village road can be detected as a hollow way with signs of house foundations to the side. Outside the boundary wall which now encloses the village you can see the ridge and furrow of the old open fields.

The land slopes down towards the river Gwash, north of the village site and there is a bridge linking Gunthorpe to Martinsthorpe. It is likely that there was a mill hereabouts in medieval times. Also, the main road between Oakham and Uppingham may have passed through the two villages and across the river here. Certainly the road has changed course during the last 500 years. One reason for the desertion of both villages may have been the change of course of the main road, though more likely is the usual depopulation due to either emparking or enclosure for sheep pasture.

**Brooke** is one of Rutland's loveliest villages, although it is so small that there is not much to see of it. The church of St Peter is the outstanding feature to meet you as you turn the corner into the village, with its 13th century tower of contrasting stones. Inside it is mainly 12th century with Elizabethan fittings and the north aisle is also of this period, when rebuilding took place in 1579. The beautiful Early English lancet window, the Norman doorway, the box pews (with their historic graffiti), the old door with its primitive hinges and the alabaster tomb of Charles Noel (1619) are some of the treasures to look for.

The village is shrunken but not deserted, although it was much larger when the Augustinian priory existed. This was founded in about 1150 and was located ½ mile to the north west along the Oakham road. All that remains today are the very considerable earthworks, but these make very distinctive landscape features and there were important alterations to the river. Since the earthworks virtually link up to the present village it must have been almost continuous. In fact, a hollow way can be seen leading from the present village towards the monastic site.

A house, now known as Brooke Priory, occupies part of the old monastic site and is used as a preparatory school at present. The Noel family purchased the manor of Brooke in the 1540s and built a fine house near to the former priory, no doubt using some of the stones for their building. Little remains of this house but a porter's lodge and gateway arch, converted into a dovecote in the 18th century. There are also some remains of the formal gardens of the late 16th and early 17th centuries.

**Gunthorpe Hall** and a number of associated buildings are all that remain of a former village which was mentioned in a forest perambulation in 1218, but its chapel was in ruins by 1534, and in 1665 the Hearth Tax shows only one resident, Anthony Sherwood. James Wright in his 'History & Antiquities of the County of Rutland', writing in 1684, says 'Gunthorp is now onely the name of certain Grounds . . . Yet here was formerly a Village, tho at present not the least sign of a Town remaining . . .' The tithe map of 1844 shows only one farm which is close to the site of the hall, built subsequently. Your walk takes you behind Gunthorpe Hall and if you have time you can see the earthworks of the former village 300 yards down the drive on the left.

**Manton** has many fine houses and cottages of ironstone and blue limestone, mainly of the 17th century. The old hall has a striking 18th century front of seven bays, but the star attraction must be St Mary's 'homely, lovable, growing gradually and comfortably but oddly elephantine in its hipped roof', according to Pevsner. Look for the haphazard outlines, the early 13th century west front with its 'eye of the needle' window, its Rutland-style bell cote, its font of 1200, about the date of the original church, with a rebuilt chancel of 1795. By the way, Manton sits on top of the railway tunnel of the main Birmingham-Leicester-Peterborough line.

# Uppingham and Lyddington

**Introduction:** This walk explores the lovely countryside of south Rutland, giving excellent views over the Welland valley towards Rockingham Castle and Northamptonshire. It starts in the vintage market town of Uppingham with its world-famous public school and crosses the fields to Lyddington, one of Rutland's most outstandingly beautiful villages with ironstone cottages, a green and, next to the church, the former palace of the Bishops of Lincoln, now the Bedehouse. Nearby, you can walk through a small tower called the Bishop's Eye along the precinct wall.

A short distance to the west lies the small, almost secret, village of Stoke Dry, overlooking Rutland's forgotten Eye Brook Reservoir. Inside the remarkable church of St Andrew you will find wall paintings, monuments and carvings displaying unique features. Was the Gunpowder Plot hatched in the small room over the North Porch?

As you return to Uppingham climbing the steep-sided Eye Brook valley you have splendid views of the woodlands which are the remaining evidence of the Royal Forest of Leighfield, once straddling the wild border between Leicestershire and Rutland and running into the extensive Rockingham Forest.

**Distance:** The walk is about 7 miles and takes approximately 3½ hours to complete, but allow some extra time to visit the church and Bedehouse at Lyddington, Stoke Dry church, some birdwatching at Eye Brook Reservoir and a look around Uppingham. OS Landranger 141.

**Refreshments:** There are excellent pubs, cafes and restaurants in Uppingham. In Lyddington there are the Marquess of Exeter and White Hart pubs.

**How to get there:** Uppingham is near the junction of the A47 and A6003. If approaching from the A6003 direction all you need to do is to turn right into South View (below the church) as you enter

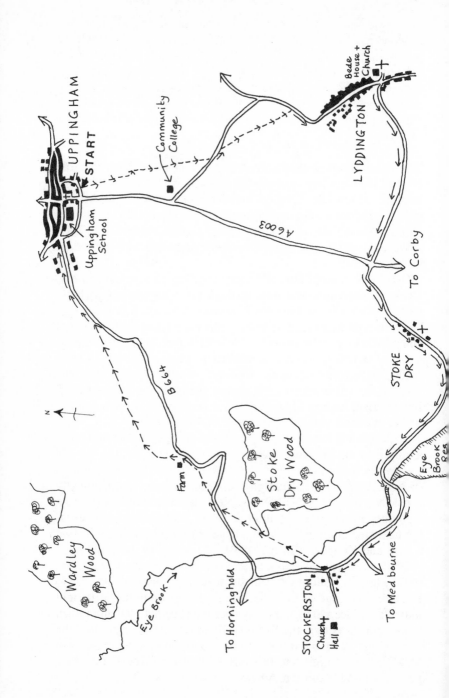

the town. Park in this road. If approaching from the A47 roundabout out of town, take the A6003 turning into Uppingham, go through the town (traffic lights) and downhill past the church (on your left). Turn left into South View at the crossroads at the foot of the hill. Park in South View. Alternatively, there are car parks signposted elsewhere in town if you prefer, from which you would walk the short distance to South View, on the southern edge of town.

**The Walk:** Start in South View at the footpath sign, just a little beyond the cemetery. Follow the slightly overgrown path which borders allotments. Cross a stile and look for yellow arrows marking the route. Go over a small stream via a plank. Cross the sheep pasture field and pause at the top of the hill to look back at the view of Uppingham situated on a ridge and with the school buildings to the left.

Cross over a metal stile and keep to the side of a ploughed field. Cross another stile and pass through an overgrown and partly wooded area. On reaching a narrow lane, turn left, follow the sign and turn right in 50 yards. Cross a stile and go downhill to another stile. Usually no stream is visible unless heavy rain has fallen.

Carry on uphill over a stile marked by arrows and into a school field (Uppingham Community College). Aim for the telegraph pole and the far left corner of the school field. At the gate turn left into the road leading to Lyddington. Excellent views now emerge of the Welland valley and, on the skyline, Corby.

Continue left for about 200 yards and at the footpath sign cross a stile into the ploughed field on the right. Go towards the ash tree in the field. Cross a stile into the next field looking again at the lovely views of Lyddington in front of you. Go diagonally across the pasture field, cross a fence and stile and then through a ploughed field to a stile at the far side. Proceed into and across the next field aiming for the opposite corner where you will find a stile and signpost. Go into the lane leading to the village.

Walk to the village green, cross to the far corner in the direction of the church. Follow the pathway leading to the Bedehouse. Go through a passage at the side leading to the church. Turn right into a lane. Keep to the pathway near the precinct wall and return to the main street via the Bishop's Eye tower. Turn right into the main street and carry on until you reach the lane signposted to Stoke Dry. Turn left into this following it for about 1 mile until you reach and cross the A6003.

Proceed downhill into St Andrew's church, Stoke Dry, then down the same lane to the shore of the Eye Brook Reservoir. Bear right following the road alongside the reservoir, crossing the bridge over the Eye Brook stream and turn sharp right to Stockerston. There are many places to pause along the shoreline.

Take care as you reach the junction with the Medbourne road as this can be busy with traffic. Proceed straight on for 300 yards to a row of cottages on the right. Look for a footpath sign here and go alongside the last cottage, over a gate and into a field. Cross the field to a bridge over a stream. Ahead there is an iron gate and a well-marked path on the left. Take this track and look for a large iron gate 200 yards further on to the right. Go through onto rough ground. Turn left into the trees for a small wooden gate. Go through it into a cornfield and cross diagonally to the opposite corner aiming for a solitary oak tree.

You now reach the B664 from Stockerston to Uppingham (which you were on before for a while). Follow it for a short distance until you reach the oak tree and field gate on the left. Go into and across the ploughed field towards a clump of trees ahead. This area is known as King's Hill.

You emerge onto the main road again and follow this for 300 yards only until you reach an iron gate and farm track on the left leading to a silage tower. Bear right to another iron gate following yellow arrow signs for 100 yards. Continue along the hedge until you reach a stile then cross into a ploughed field. There are very fine views of Wardley Wood and Wardley village.

Cross another stile (arrow) into a pasture field then diagonally across to an ash tree, over a plank bridge and stile (arrow). On to a double stile and plank across a ditch. Now you will see two spires ahead of you marking the location of Uppingham.

Cross the next field diagonally to another double stile and ditch (arrow), across a field to a gap in the hedge, then, finally across a field towards bungalows following the path to a stile and the main road.

You proceed straight into the town passing the Uppingham School swimming pool and theatre on the left as well as several boarding houses on the right. Eventually you reach High Street West with the main school buildings on the right, including the impressive gateway. You will soon be in the market place. Go to the church door, turn left and follow the path round. The old building on the left with Latin and Hebrew inscriptions is the original Uppingham School of 1584, now used as an art room.

Turn left again, round the side of the old school, passing also the village pound on your right. You enter an open space with seats where you can rest awhile and this is South View where you began the walk.

## Historical Notes

**Uppingham** sits on a ridge and the long High Street extends through the town. In fact, it is such a long street that it has to be divided into High Street West and High Street East. The market place is still the focus of the town with the church of St Peter and St Paul standing guard over it. Its 14th century tower, big-angled buttresses and tall recessed spire are a landmark from afar. Like so many buildings around it, the church is built of the warm brown ironstone quarried locally from 'the Pits' and 'Humpty Dumpty Fields'. Look also for corners and facades which may be made from the grey Lincolnshire Limestone.

As you stand near Queen Victoria's Jubilee fountain facing the church you will see on your right the late 18th century building, now the post office, with interesting window and door details. The shambles, successively slaughter house, butchery then fire station, were once on the site of the present toilets. In front of you is the long-established Vaults but the White Swan, once nearby, has now vanished. The church porch invites visitors since it leads directly from the market square.

On your left the Midland Bank has an attractive fancy Jacobean front with much carving and is the result of rebuilding gabled premises in 1900. There is a good 19th century shop window further round, at the corner.

When you turn round to look at the famous old coaching inn, the Falcon Hotel, you notice how it dominates the square. One hundred years ago the whole front looked very different. The Victorian gables were absent; there was an archway passage, now the main entrance to the hotel and blocked in. The passage led to an extensive backyard, which like so many Uppingham backways, is well worth a visit. You will find that several of these backways have now been attractively converted to shops and restaurants.

The Uppingham Bookshop was a garage in the 1930s and it has recently undergone extensive alterations whilst successfully retaining its impressive facade. There is still an active cattle and sheep market as well as the Friday market stalls. Once bull-baiting took place here with farm carts arranged round the square for spectators. There were two fairs in March and July, now there is an Uppingham Feast Day.

If you follow a pathway around the church to the left of the market square entrance you will come to the original Uppingham school building of 1584, founded by Archdeacon Robert Johnson 'because there is no free grammer school for instructing boys in sound learning in our county of Rutland he has begged us to think fit to erect, found and establish one grammer school in the town of Okeham and another in the town of Uppingham for the better education, institution and instruction of boys and youths dwelling and residing in the aforesaid places'. This is used as the art room of Uppingham school, but the main school buildings are to be found in High Street West. Here you will find School Lane and a fine gateway there. Further along the street there is an even more imposing gateway, much like a Cambridge college. Indeed, if you peep into either gateway you will notice the quadrangle and buildings, including the school chapel, reminiscent of Oxbridge. Look for the statue of the great headmaster, Edward Thring, outside the chapel.

Many of the school boarding houses and associated buildings are scattered throughout the town and it has a great impact on the place. As you walk around you will see a harmony in the materials and styles of buildings. There will be date stones and interesting features, such as a unicorn sundial to find. Notice the fine frontage of the Exeter Arms. For the book lover there are several antiquarian bookshops and also a fine art gallery.

**Lyddington** lies in a secluded side valley of the river Welland. It is often called Long Lyddington as the lovely ironstone buildings extend almost a mile along the main street. There are many fine 17th century houses; for example, the Priest's House (1626) and a house dated at 1674 north of the green. The village cross stood on the green but in 1837 a gang of navvies making the nearby turnpike road pulled it down and it was not until 1930 that the stump of the 15th century cross-shaft was replaced near its former site.

For many centuries the village was a centre for the bishops of Lincoln. Since the Lincoln Diocese was so large the Bishops needed to establish palaces where they could stay. One of these was in Lyddington at the building later known as the Bedehouse. This stands next to the church of St Andrew and a precinct wall with its watch tower or Bishop's Eye is nearby. Behind this lovely grouping of buildings are the remains of extensive fishponds used by the bishops. Since the bishops were also interested in hunting, a large deer park was enclosed in the area from the 13th century and some names such as 'Long Park' on the map are a reminder of this.

The present Bedehouse has been restored. Inside, look for the fine hall, the exquisite 400 year old ceiling of panelled oak with rich carving, the heraldic glass, splendid fireplaces and richly-moulded doorways. The palace was turned into an almshouse in 1602 by the Cecils who had recently acquired it. This family, the Earls of Exeter, based at Burghley House, Stamford, owned much land in Rutland. The building was used as an almshouse until the 1930s and is described by Astley V. Clarke as 'one of the finest specimens of 15th century domestic architecture in the country'. Open April-September, daily 10 am-1 pm and 2-6 pm.

**St Andrew's church** has a massive 14th century tower 'crowned by an ill-proportioned spire'. The present nave and aisles were built in the 15th century and the chancel 14th century when the floor appears to have been raised. The perpendicular arcades of the nave with moulded arches, dignified piers and large clerestory windows give spaciousness and beautiful lighting to the church. There is a 15th century rood screen, remains of wall-painting, acoustic jars aimed at amplifying the parson's voice, coffin slabs and fine brasses to Heleyn Hardy (1486) and Edward Watson (1530).

The altar stands away from the east wall and is surrounded on four sides by the communion rails. This is a compromise between Archbishop Laud who wanted altars at the east end and the Puritans who wanted the altar table further towards the congregation.

**Stoke Dry** still has considerable woodland in its vicinity which is a reminder of earlier times when Rockingham Forest and Leighfield Forest came together in this place. High and dry above the Eye Brook, this very small village has views over a wide area but itself may not be so easily seen from some quarters. West of the crossroads, which you pass, there were six quarries where building stone for Lyddington and Stoke Dry was obtained in the past.

St Andrew's is 'a most lovable church', off the beaten track with 'Barbaric art . . . entirely uncomposed . . . full of vitality and zest'. Its curious features include fine carved columns and capitals where you can search for the Devil, dragons, lions and an eagle as well as a rare bishop-like figure with wings. There is a 15th century rood screen still retaining the coving for its loft, a late 17th century communion rail, wall paintings showing the crucifixion of St Andrew, the murder of St Thomas Becket and the martyrdom of St Edmund. Look for the Danish archer, and is that really a Red Indian wearing the well-known head-dress? Surely not.

There are monuments to the Digby family who came to Stoke Dry in the 15th century until the end of the 17th century. The most famous monument is that of Kenelm Digby in 16th century armour with his 11 children around him. The room over the north porch is a parvise or priest's room which legend suggests was one of the locations where the Gunpowder Plotters met. Since Sir Everard Digby was implicated in the plot and executed for his part in it in 1606 this may not be entirely far-fetched. There is an excellent oriel window you should see.

**The Eye Brook Reservoir** was constructed to supply water to the steelworks in Corby. Work began in June 1936 and the reservoir filled by December 1940, supplying raw water to the Corby works on 31st December, 1940. This was the first time a large natural impounding reservoir had been built on very fertile ground in Eastern England. A total of 400 acres of best beef-raising grassland had been covered by water. Some afforestation took place around the reservoir, a trout farm was developed and a bird sanctuary established (later to be declared a SSSI). Some water had to be supplied to the locality, namely Kettering, Market Harborough, Uppingham and Wellingborough. Now, less than 50 years after the construction and filling of the reservoir, steel making in Corby has ceased, though some ancillary work remains. Service industries based on large industrial estates have taken over.

**Stockerston** is close to the Eye Brook but far enough away to avoid flooding which would have occurred in the past. Also, once deep in the heart of the forest, it is still surrounded by well-known woods such as Great Merrible, Bolt Wood, Allexton Wood and Wardley Wood. St Peter's church 'lovely and atmospheric' has a beautiful setting outside the village and is close to a small Georgian hall, linked by pleasant pathways. It is well worth making the short diversion up a country lane to see them.